Decorating Time Savers

Decorating Time Savers

Jack Warner

Rutledge Books, Inc.

Danbury, CT

Cover design by Ivy Calahorrano

Interior design by Kelly Rothen

Rutledge Books, Inc.
107 Mill Plain Road, Danbury, CT 06811
1-800-278-8533
www.rutledgebooks.com

Manufactured in the United States of America

Cataloging in Publication Data
Warner, Jack

Decorating Time Savers

ISBN: 1-58244-190-1

1. Creative home decorating. 2. How to tips — save time and money. 3. Workable plans.

Library of Congress Control Number: 2001091645

Contents

PART II *Planning Guides*

Section I *Detailed By Room*

Section 2 ***Detailed By Category***

Appendix (Web Sites Worth Visiting)

Foreward: How to use this book

This book is divided into two major parts.

Part I *Decorating Time Savers*
Shows you how to organize your ideas and actions to realize your decorating goals swiftly with a minimum amount of anxiety, shopping time and expense. You'll find it full of practical suggestions. . . for deciding the "look" and style for each room, the best floor plans, color schemes, lighting, accessories, etc.

Then it shows you how to organize the whole buying process to save lots of time, money and frustration. You'll learn to buy like a pro and to avoid those repeated, time-consuming trips back to the mall to get all those items you still need or have somehow forgotten.

Part II *Planning Guides*
In this section, you'll find structured buying lists to help you pre-plan, organize, and speed up the acquisition of those hundreds of items needed to completely furnish your home. First, they'll help you remember dozens of items you might initially forget. And secondly, and far more important, with them you'll become an efficient professional buyer deserving the personal assistance of store management, rather than just an ignored shopper searching for hours through stacks of merchandise and standing in long checkout lines.

The overall goal of this book
To help you create a fully furnished home or apartment that you'll love that's 100% complete just weeks after you start.

After all, you have too much to do and enjoy in this life to let decorating become a prolonged preoccupation and irritant. Besides, it's no fun and a perpetual distraction to have to live in a "work in progress".

PART I

Decorating Time Savers

1. How this book came to be written

Necessity was the driving force behind the development of the ideas expressed in this book.

It all started several years ago when my wife and I made an offer on a charming new 3-bedroom house on Nantucket Island off Cape Cod in Massachusetts. We thought it would be a great investment—giving us good rental income, strong long-term appreciation, and the chance to use the house ourselves for the two weeks that tax laws then allowed.

After our offer was accepted and we signed the purchase and sale agreement, the shocker came when our realtor told us that we should try to have the house fully furnished and decorated by December 1 to assure a full slate of rentals for the following season. December 1 was little more than a month after the planned closing! And this was an empty 3-bedroom house more than 8 hours distant (including a ferryboat ride of over two hours) from our home in New Jersey! Yes, there were a few high-end decorators on the island, and even a furniture store or two, but our budget and the timing constraints ruled them out.

Once the initial panic passed, we realized that the short lead-time was only part of the problem. Because of the great distance and lack of local stores open on the island year round, we'd have to select and buy everything that we needed in advance in the New York/New Jersey area. We'd have to accumulate and store it all in our house and garage, and then on the appointed day load it all into a big rental truck for our long trek to Nantucket. Only after it was unloaded, unwrapped, and put into place would we see how everything worked together. There'd be no chance to start out with a few items, see how they looked together, then add more and more items to complete our decorating.

All our decisions had to be made up-front—from big things like furniture, rugs and draperies—to important things like lamps and wall hangings—to little things like placemats, ice buckets, fire extinguishers and even a corkscrew. Little wonder we called our targeted departure day "D-Day." It would take only a little less planning than the landing at Normandy!

How then to do it quickly and "right the first time" while also working full time? Fortunately, the answers came from adopting some of the same techniques that I'd used many times before in my ad agency work. Often, on impossibly short notice, we'd have to fully design, build and dress a set for a complex TV or photo shoot. Often, within a single day, we'd have to transform space in an empty convention hall into a fully functioning 10,000-square-foot trade show exhibit. And before that, back in college, we'd routinely design and build all our stage sets for a major school production in just weeks. And four times a year, we'd convert our yawning field house into a themed fantasy setting for gala proms, attended by more than 1,000 students. All it took then, and would take now, is a creative concept, a detailed action plan, and lots of lists to make sure that everything came together on the appointed day.

So, adopting these techniques, we began the process. All our planning was done before the actual house closing. (We decided to buy nothing earlier than that date in case the deal fell through.) Then immediately after the closing, the buying began. Everything worked. We were ready for D-Day, and the completed house looked great. This was to be our first experience in what was then still a 60-day decorating process.

The whole experience was so enjoyable (and profitable), that two years later we tried it again—this time with a larger and more formal 3-bedroom house adjacent to our first one in Nantucket. Learning from our first experience and armed with our starter lists, this time we were able to complete everything in just under 45 days.

Then two years later, we got back into the Nantucket real estate market, this time purchasing a sprawling 4-bedroom, 4-bath house on a 6-acre lot. Not intended for rental, this house was to become our summer retirement home. Building on our experience with the first two houses, we fully decorated and furnished this one in exactly 30 days. In fact, on that thirtieth day we held a fun "wrap party" in our new house to thank our builder, his crew and our realtor. And frankly, it was at their urging during this party, that this book eventually came to be written. Astonished that things had been accomplished so well and so fast, they prompted us to share our ideas (and our lists) with others.

There's more to this story. In fact, it's ongoing. Using the same techniques, we fully re-did several rooms in our New Jersey house—including the kitchen, the entire third floor, a home office and basement. And next year, we plan to turn an unused detached garage into a studio/workshop.

Even after all this time, I can honestly say that it's more fun than ever! Principally because we get things to come out exactly like we want—without all those frustrating hours searching through the malls and shuttling back and forth with "on approval" purchases. We've learned that becoming "30-day decorators" is only partly about saving time. Even more important, it's given us a decision-making discipline that's led to better decisions and far better outcomes.

2. Do you really want to live in a "work in progress"?

How often have you heard friends complain, with a weak smile, that they're still living out of cartons six months or more after their move into a new house or apartment?

How often have you visited a friend's new place only to hear them explain, with a slightly embarrassed shrug, that they haven't had the time yet to pick out new furniture, or new draperies, or new lamps, or new rugs, or the right things to hang on the wall?

And when it's your new place, how often have you come home, gazed across those still half-empty rooms, and wished that magically somehow everything was finished—so that you could stop feeling guilty and could forget about it?

Let's face it, like most of your friends, you're far too busy to make shopping and decorating an ongoing priority. From the beginning, you deserve and need a home that's a comforting haven where you can relax, recharge and entertain—rather than an unsettled distraction and an ongoing guilt trip.

In short, it's not fun and not necessary to live in a "work in progress" surrounded by boxes and half-empty rooms. Not when you can have everything the way you want it within a week of moving in. All it takes to start, is overcoming the four obstacles covered in the next chapter.

3. Obstacles to action
• time
• money
• self-confidence
• a game plan

All four of these obstacles conspire to make most people drag out their decorating decisions. (The exceptions are those well-heeled few who throw in the towel up front and call in a decorator.) But for most of us on a budget, those *Architectural Digest*-style rooms are just out of the question. So we have to do it ourselves, which at first can seem a bit overwhelming. But it really needn't be, once you step back and organize your thinking. Plus, doing it all yourself can be great fun and a continual source of satisfaction and pride. Doing it all yourself assures that your home reflects your own personal tastes and unique personality, rather than just making you a resident in some other person's creative vision.

So let's tackle each of these four obstacles head on to resolve them.

• **Time** Obviously it takes time to select and buy the hundreds of items needed for a well-equipped home. But it'll take far, far longer if you stretch out your acquisition of those items over a several month (or year) period. Those back-and-forth trips to the mall for a single item or two will consume enormous amounts of your time, enthusiasm and energy. The ongoing frustration can even weary you to the point of no longer really caring.

Approach decorating the same way you plan a dinner party. You decide whom to invite, what to serve and what you need at the market to pull it all together. Armed with a carefully-made list, you pick up everything in less than two hours. Then you get busy in the kitchen. They arrive at the appointed hour. And you all have a great time together.

Contrast that with the way most people approach decorating—as a sequence of step-by-step decisions. If you used that same process for a dinner party, here's what would happen. You'd go out to the market, look around, and maybe buy a chicken or a rib roast. You'd go home and think about what might go well with it. You'd then run out for rice or potatoes, and later run out for vegetables. After that you'd make repeated trips to the stores for your appetizers, salad fixings, dessert, rolls, wine, etc. All this would take so long that there'd be little time to do a really imaginative job of food preparation. When your guests did arrive, for a nice but just OK dinner, you'd be so tired that you couldn't enjoy the evening.

The "not enough time" obstacle to decorating action is based on a natural fear that the whole process will become a massive, ongoing, all-consuming effort. But that just won't be the case if you shortcut the process with effective planning.

A weekend and maybe a few evenings of planning nails down just about all the key elements to get you started. Then you draw up your lists (using Part II of this book) and head out to start buying, armed with new knowledge on how to buy smartly and efficiently like a pro.

With these lists, you'll find that even the most compulsive and impatient shoppers will derive great satisfaction as they record their rapid success—as they check off more and more of the "Have" boxes on their buying lists.

• **Money** New furniture and furnishings do cost money, but chances are fairly certain that today's prices are lower than they'll be in the future. Also, by setting your total decorating budget at the outset, you'll make far more cost-effective decisions throughout the whole process. For example, if you decide you can spend no more than $4,000 on your living room, you'll resist spending $3,500 on that fantastic sofa—because you'll know that it will just have to sit there with little else in the room for two years or more, unless you go way, way, over your planned budget. The same principle applies whether your living room budget is $4,000 or $40,000. Front-end planning helps you save money by buying smarter.

Also, when you group your purchases (as described in chapter 12), you'll secure better prices and larger discounts. This lets you accomplish even more with the same budget.

The "not enough money" obstacle to decorating action is based on a natural fear that the whole spending process will spiral out of control. But that won't be the case if you manage the process thoughtfully.

Obviously, if you have no money at all because you've spent everything on your down payment and closing costs, you do have a real problem. You're forced to not buy anything new until you've built up some savings or can swing a home equity loan. Until then, use this book to do all your front-end planning, including the preparation of your lists. Then when you do have the budget you'll be ready to go!

• **Self confidence** Frankly, the main reason that most people stretch out their decorating decisions is an underlying fear that despite all the time, money and effort, things just won't turn out right. So they take tentative mini-steps, rather than bold ones.

This often unrecognized fear is fed by glossy magazine articles and books by design professionals. They show us a $50,000 room with fancy fabrics, custom pieces and one-of-a-kind accessories to dazzle us with their marvelous taste and great creativity. Most times, you don't really like the room all that much anyway, so you increasingly wonder what chance do you have when even the pros miss the mark so often.

And far too often, the rooms you do love provide you with unattainable models. Either because of your room's basic architectural differences, your lack of those impossible-to-find accessories, or your lack of a big budget.

When you strip away all the mystique, decorating is nothing more than basic nest building. And it's your nest you're decorating, so you'll know by instinct what'll make you feel snug, comfortable and happy. Don't let those decorating magazines and books intimidate you. Most of the rooms shown in them were assembled to impress and to photograph, not really to live in. (It may surprise you to learn that many of the homes of the rich and famous, shown in magazines, were specially propped just for the photo shoots. Decorators arrived with a truckload of special pieces, which were removed right after the photo session ended. Pretty tricky!)

We've already discussed why buying everything up front will save you time and money. An added benefit is that it will almost assure that everything will work well together. The reason is that most manufacturers and stores feature design-coordinated collections. Their designers and buyers have pre-assembled a large and fully compatible range of great pieces. If you like what you see, you can mix and match the items in that collection to accomplish your specific goals. If you don't like what you see, you can move along to another store with a collection you like.

• **A Game Plan** "So much to do. So little time. Where to begin? Maybe I'd better wait until next week when I have more time to think about this!" That little thought sequence is a rationalization that shoves your planning back week after week. And it typifies another major obstacle to decorating action—the lack of a sound game plan.

Obviously, anything as major as a top-to-bottom decorating project takes a game plan to optimize your efforts. And that's exactly what this book gives you. Just read on and get started.

Where to start — •tape measure •camera •and graph paper

In a single intensive session, you can record all the information you need to prepare good measured drawings for each room and area in your project. If you can gain the owner's permission, do this even before you've closed the deal to purchase or lease the space. This lets you do all your early planning up front.

It's also a good idea to take wide-angle photographs of each room, along with detailed close-ups. If you don't have a camera with a 25-mm wide-angle lens, borrow or rent one. With a lens this wide you'll be able to squeeze most of the room into your shots. Typically, you'll want to take shots from each corner of the room, as well as straight on for each wall. Also, take close-ups to record the details of moldings, windows, doors, mantels, radiators, and built-ins like bookcases. And don't forget closet interiors. The idea is to get full documentation so that you don't have to go any further than your measured drawings and photographs once you start planning.

For my documentation photographs, I prefer to use black and white film. This eliminates the existing colors, and makes it easier to visualize new ones. That's important, especially if the room I'm photographing is already furnished. If there are colored areas I can't or don't want to change, such as stained-glass windows, tiled or carpeted floors, or marble fireplace surrounds, I shoot these areas in color as well as in black and white.

When you take measurements, do the walls as well as the floors. How high are the windowsills off the floor? How big is the space above the windows and the doors? How wide are the trim moldings for both? How tall are the baseboards, the radiators, etc.? Where and how big are the electrical outlets, wall switches, sconces, etc.? And if there are hanging fixtures, beams or soffits, take measurements for your ceilings too.

Because you'll eventually have to order window treatments (shades, blinds, curtains, drapes and/or valances) be sure to take precise measurements for each window too. You'll find worksheets on pages 15 and 16 that will allow you to consolidate this information from your rough worksheets.

As you take measurements, it's not necessary to do scale drawings on site. You can do that later with graph paper at home. Just make a rough sketch of the floor plan and each wall—showing the general placement of windows, doors, etc. Then go to work with your tape measure, jotting down all the key measurements on your rough sketch. But be sure to label each sheet clearly, so that you'll know which wall goes where in your final drawings.

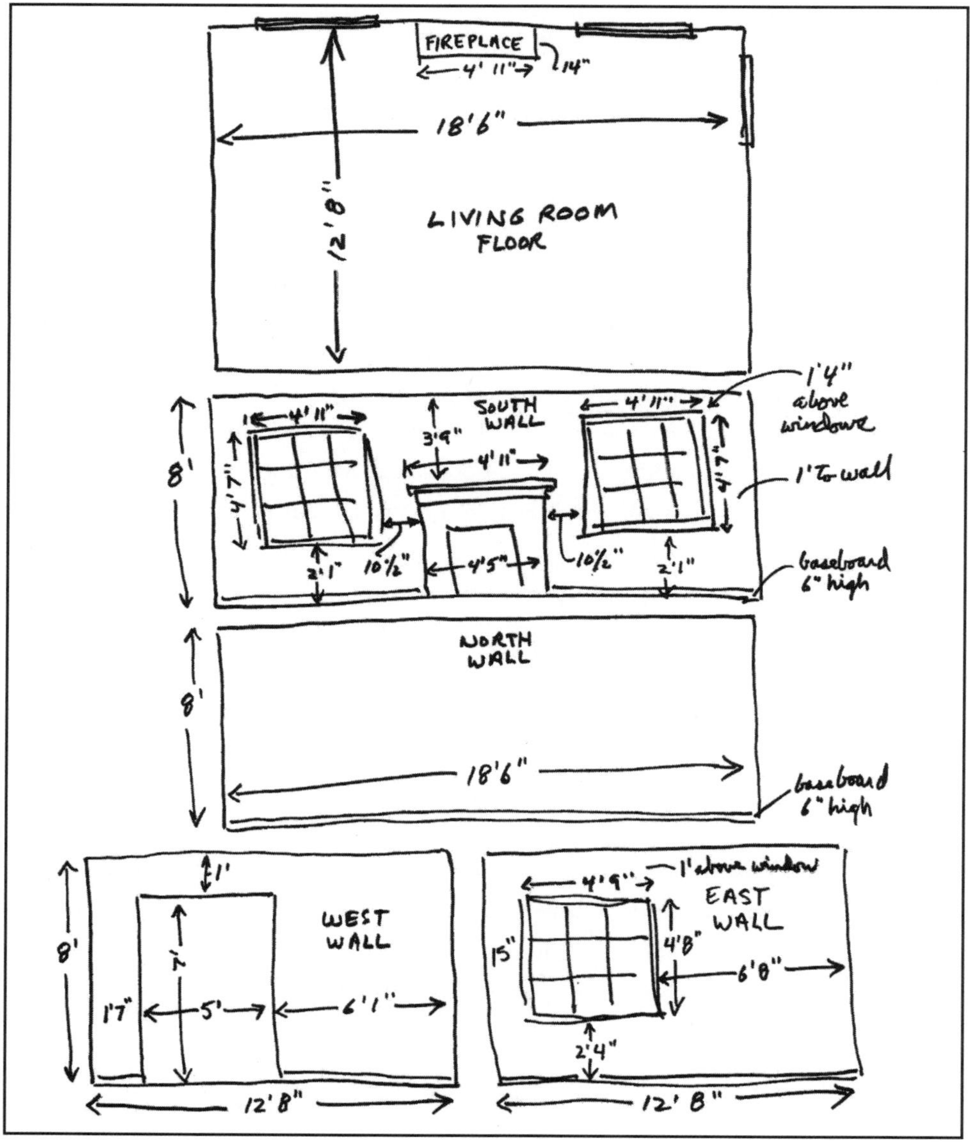

Make rough on-site sketches with measurements.

One important suggestion: If you don't already have one, invest in a good 25-foot retractable tape measure. You'll find it makes the whole measuring process go much faster.

Window measurements to record

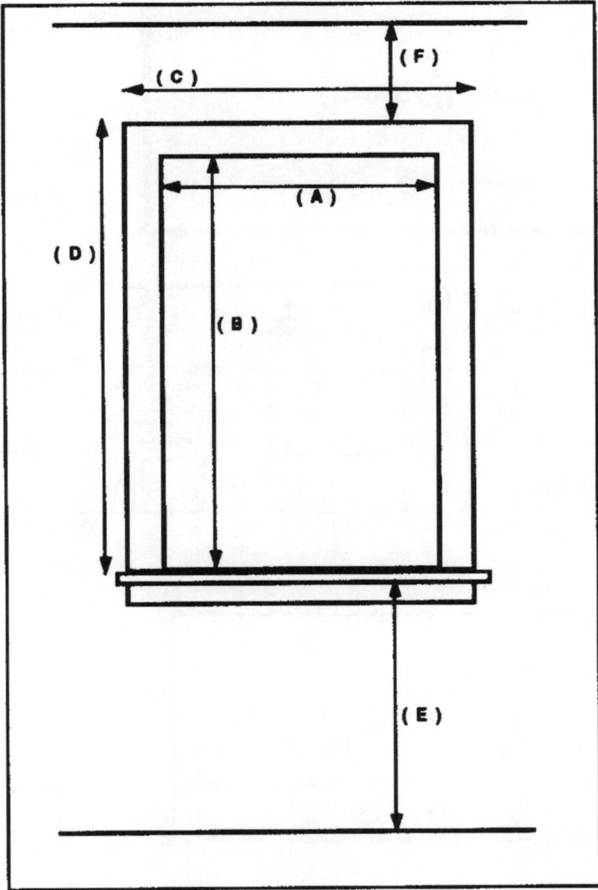

Take all the measurements for each window and then record them using the worksheets on pages 15 and 16.

Once you have all your measurements and you're back home, it's time to do your measured drawings on graph paper. A 1/4-inch-to-the-foot scale is a good one to use. Do two versions—the first with all your measurements recorded for future reference, the second with just the to-scale shapes. But in the second version, position the walls around the edges of the floor plan so that you can see everything at a glance—doors, windows, etc. Picture a shoebox with the corners slit and the sides folded down. That's the idea of this "flattened" room drawing. This is the one you'll use most in planning your decorating.

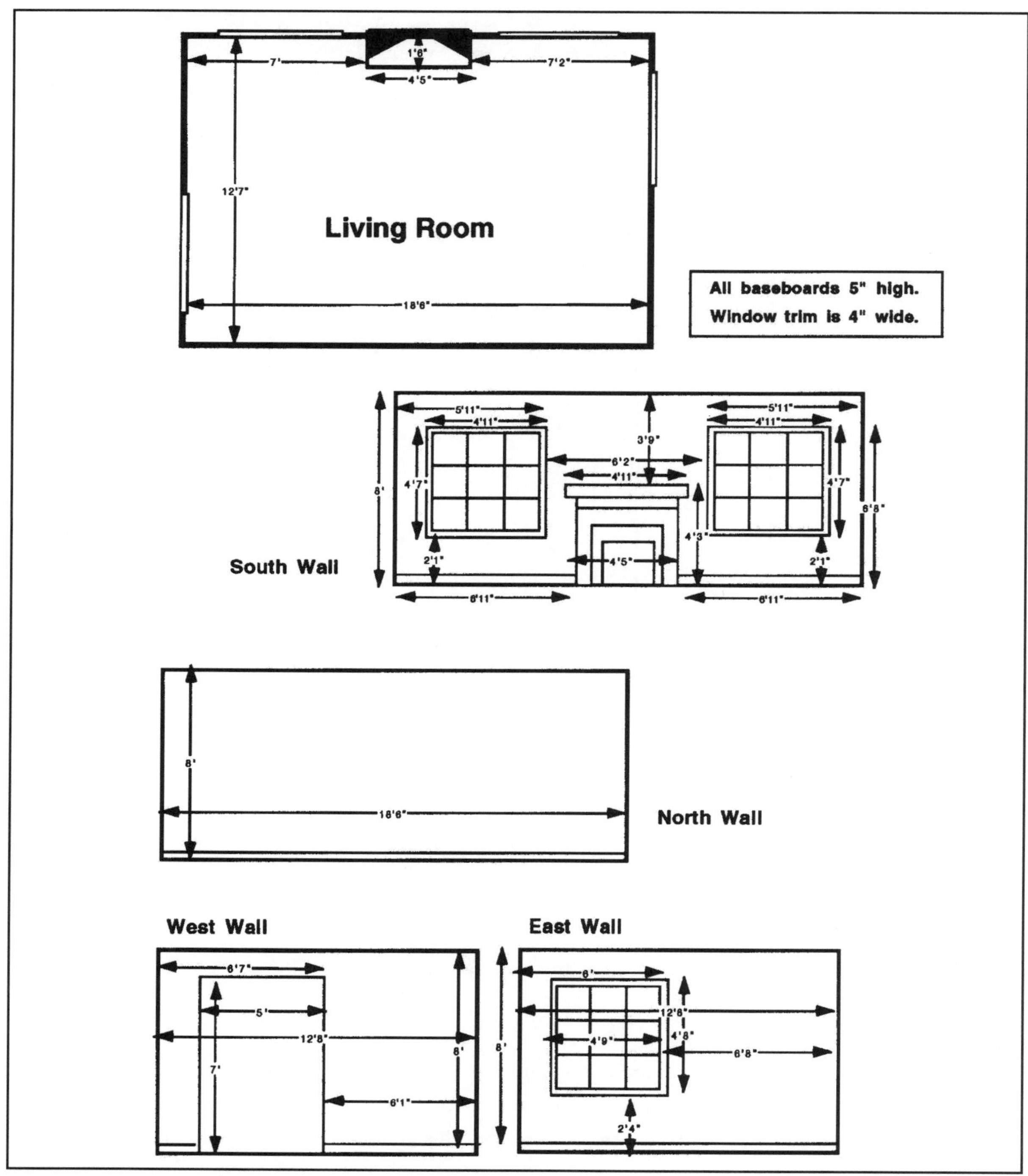

Back home, make "to-scale" drawings on graph paper with all the measurements recorded for future reference.

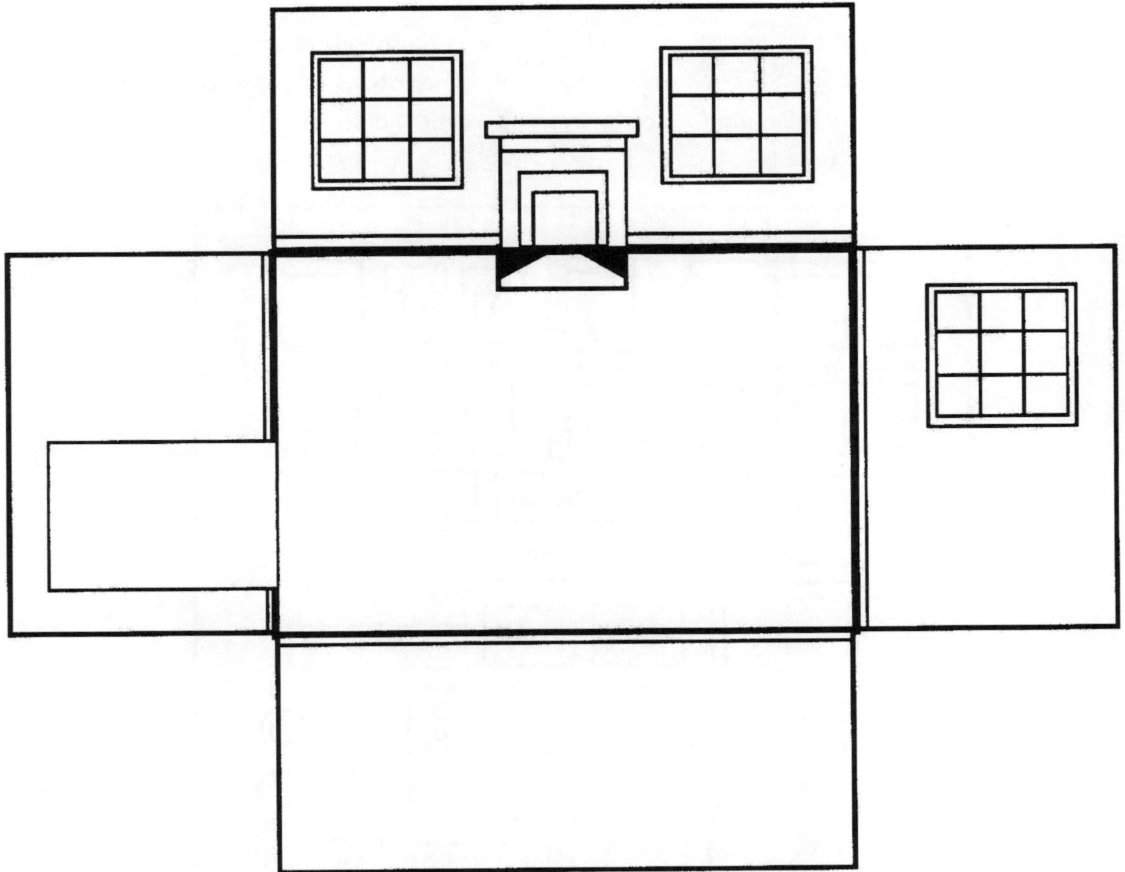

Then make to-scale "flattened" room drawings to use in planning your actual decorating. With flattened drawings, you'll be able to peer down into each room and, at a glance, see the relationship of the wall features to your floor plan.

What about furniture?

Your measured drawings should be for empty rooms. Just as black and white photography eliminates the existing colors so that you can better visualize new ones, your measured drawings should eliminate the existing furniture placement so that you can better visualize new placements.

While you're at it, do take furniture measurements too. Not only for any furniture you have that you plan to use in your new place, but also for any furniture pieces the prior owner has that seem to work particularly well. This will be a useful reference for new pieces you might want to buy.

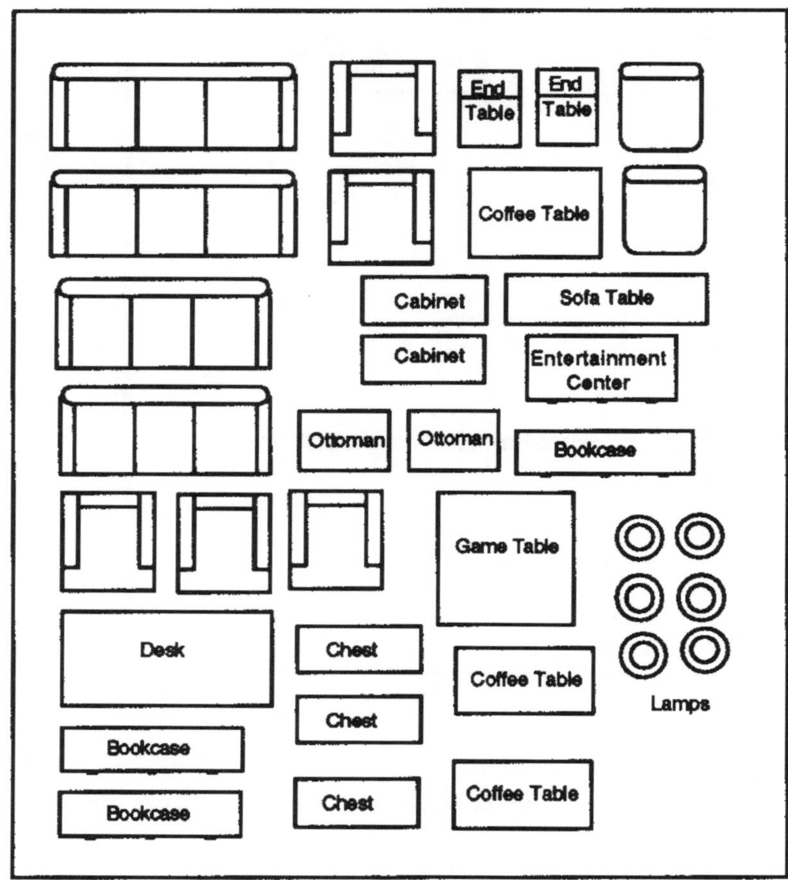

To-scale furniture drawings to clip out and position on your room drawings.

For furniture, measure the height as well as the width and depth. Later, transfer this information to graph paper, using the same 1/4-inch-to-the-foot scale you used for your room drawings. You can then make photocopies, cut them out and use them to try different arrangements on your flattened room drawings.

Window Measurements-

Room*	Window#	Inside Dimension - Width (A)	Inside Dimension - Height (B)	Outside Dimension - Width (C)	Outside Dimension - Height (D)	Sill-to - Floor (E)	Trim-to - Ceiling (F)	Treatment
A	*#1*	*27 1/4″*	*49 3/4″*	*35 1/4″*	*54″*	*30″*	*12″*	*Drapes*

*** Room Codes:**	D. Study/H. Office	H. Pantry/Utl Cl	L. Bedroom #4	P. Bath #4	T. Basement	X. Extra Rm #1
A. Living Room	E. Foyer	I. Master Bedrm	M. Master Bath	Q. Upst Hall	U. Garage	Y. Extra Rm #2
B. Dining Room	F. Hallway	J. Bedroom #2	N. Bath #2	R. Laundry Rm	V. Patio/Porch	Z. Extra Rm #3
C. Family Room	G. Kitchen	K. Bedroom #3	O. Bath #3	S. Mud Room	W. Outside	

Window Measurements-

Room*	Window#	Inside Dimension - Width (A)	Inside Dimension - Height (B)	Outside Dimension - Width (C)	Outside Dimension - Height (D)	Sill-to - Floor (E)	Trim-to - Ceiling (F)	Treatment

*** Room Codes:**
A. Living Room
B. Dining Room
C. Family Room
D. Study/H. Office
E. Foyer
F. Hallway
G. Kitchen
H. Pantry/Utl Cl
I. Master Bedrm
J. Bedroom #2
K. Bedroom #3
L. Bedroom #4
M. Master Bath
N. Bath #2
O. Bath #3
P. Bath #4
Q. Upst Hall
R. Laundry Rm
S. Mud Room
T. Basement
U. Garage
V. Patio/Porch
W. Outside
X. Extra Rm #1
Y. Extra Rm #2
Z. Extra Rm #3

5. A Virtual Reality Tour of your new home

Don't worry, I'm not going to suggest that you hook up to some fancy 3-D computer system. The Virtual Reality Tour I'm talking about takes place right in your head. And it's very doable, even if you sometimes have problems visualizing how things will look. The key is getting organized and taking things in stages. Rather than starting with a vision in your mind of a fully furnished room, apartment or house, build your way to it in a series of steps.

To start, spread out your flattened drawings and make these few basic decisions:

1. The purpose or function of each room

Just because the last owner used a room for a certain function doesn't mean that you have to, too. You might want to swap the living room and dining room, or the living room and family room. You might want to change the entryway or make one of the bedrooms a library, media room or home office. Looking over your flattened drawings and considering your needs and preferences, decide the purpose or function of each room.

2. Your basic needs for each room

Now that you've decided the function of each room, decide what furniture pieces you need in each one to make it most useful. For example: in a combination home office/guest room you'll probably need a sofa bed, a desk with two chairs, a credenza or cabinet with file drawers, a bookcase, and a place for guests to put their clothes.

Make up a list of your basic needs for each room. Forget about (until later) all the furniture pieces you already have in your current place. Obviously, you'll want to use many (if not all) of them in your new design. But don't worry about how and where to use them until a later stage.

3. What works best where?

Using your furniture needs list, make and label scale drawings for each furniture piece on graph paper.

Do this room by room, starting with your most important room. At this stage, approximate sizes are fine. You can consult the tables on pages 22, 23 and 24, which give typical sizes for most of the furniture pieces commonly needed.

Then, using your flattened drawing for that room—plus cut-outs of your furniture pieces—play around with a number of ways to arrange things. Here, you're just exploring your options and refining your thinking. Remember, there are no hard-and-fast rules on arrangements. Also, styles do change over time. If you toured a historically accurate Victorian or Arts & Crafts home, you might be surprised to see a table with chairs in the center of the living room. Its placement there made it useful for games, reading and refreshments. Historically accurate colonial-period dining rooms had all the furniture positioned around the outer walls, with the room center clear. Depending on the planned function, pieces were moved out to the center as needed. (That's one reason for the popularity of drop-leaf tables back then.) All this made the room truly multifunctional. The point is you can and should try all sorts of arrangements. Be sure to try diagonal as well as square-on arrangements.

After you see a few good ways to do things, it's time to record them on paper. You can draw them on photocopies of your flattened room drawings. Or you can rough sketch them on tracing paper (available in pads at most art supply stores) laid over your drawings.

As you work, imagine yourself walking through and using each room. Picture yourself entertaining, relaxing, or just puttering. Picture yourself in the morning, on weekends, in the evening. Picture yourself alone, with family, with friends. Where do you want your chair? What view do you want? Where do you want your TV? Keep making overlays (or photocopy versions) until you're happy with the results.

You'll probably emerge with a few different good ways to do things. Label them option 1, option 2, etc. At this stage, you may wish to consult your spouse or roommate. That way you'll emerge with some basic decisions that please you both. But keep the other options. As you move along to block out your other rooms, you may have second thoughts based on how one room flows into another.

4. Refining your room plans

After you've picked the best basic arrangement for your rooms, flesh them out with more detail. So far, you've used only the furniture items on your "needs" list. Depending on room size, you may want to add more pieces. Perhaps adding a game table, lamp table, side table, cabinet, bookcases, or more chairs. Again, visualize yourself walking through and using the room. Once you've decided, add these extra pieces to your drawing. Then, if you'd like to use area rugs, sketch them in too.

Finally, make a clean set of your final functional drawings and you're ready to move on to decisions about style, colors, furnishings, and accessories—all of which are covered in the following chapters.

What about computers?

Even if you have interior design software that lets you "walk through" a room, my suggestion is that you not use it until after you've made all your basic decisions on paper. No doubt about it, today's computer-aided design (CAD) systems are really nifty and can be great fun to use. But at the conceptual stage they can actually limit rather than aid the creative process. The reason is they keep you too preoccupied with details too soon. That's my experience and opinion. Start with a pencil and your hand-drawn flattened room drawings. Later, you can use your computer to amaze your spouse and dazzle your friends.

There are many ways to arrange your furniture pieces. Experiment with them all on paper before deciding which version you'd most like to live in. Below and on the next two pages, you'll see four options for the same living room.

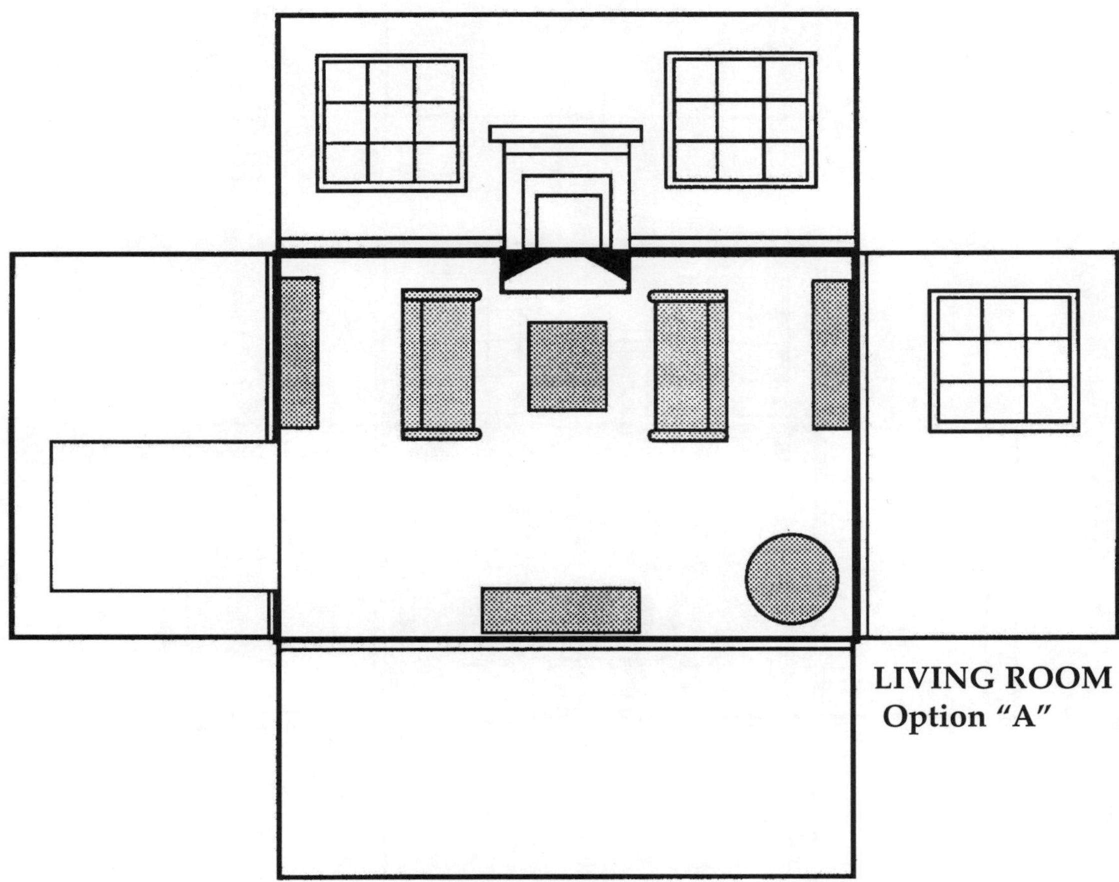

LIVING ROOM
Option "A"

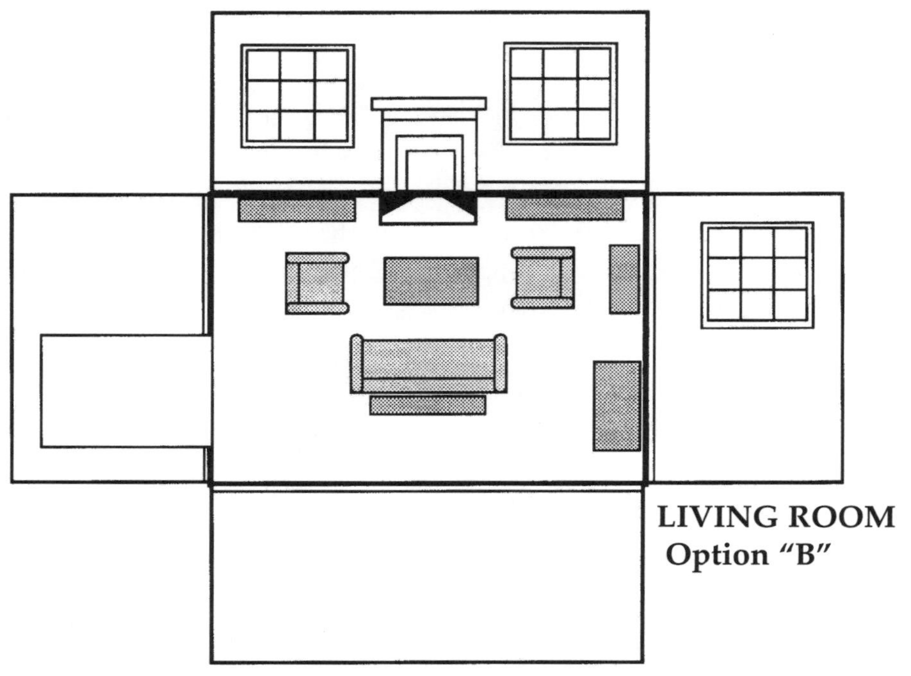

LIVING ROOM
Option "B"

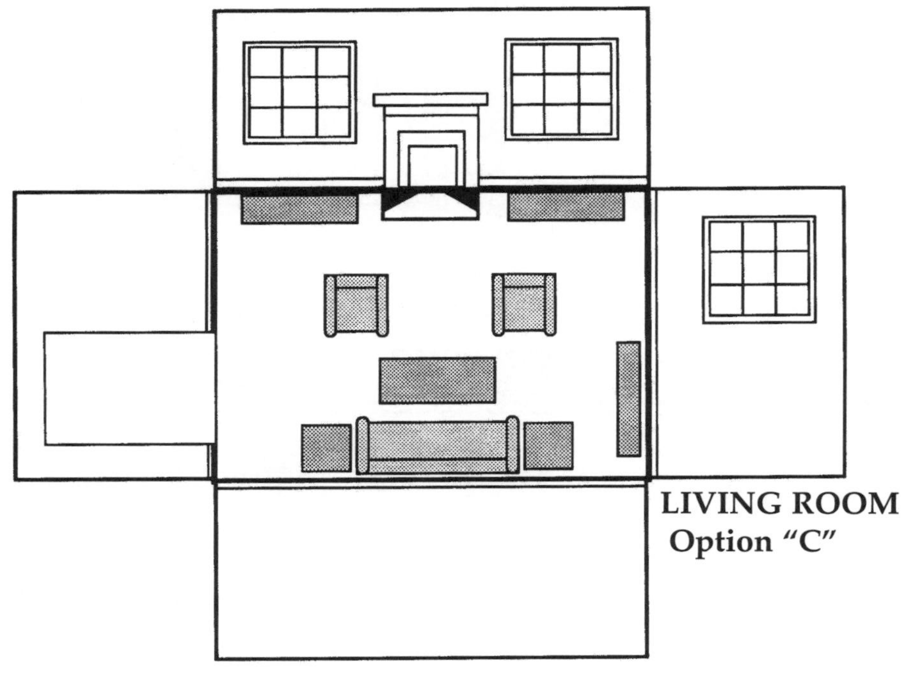

LIVING ROOM
Option "C"

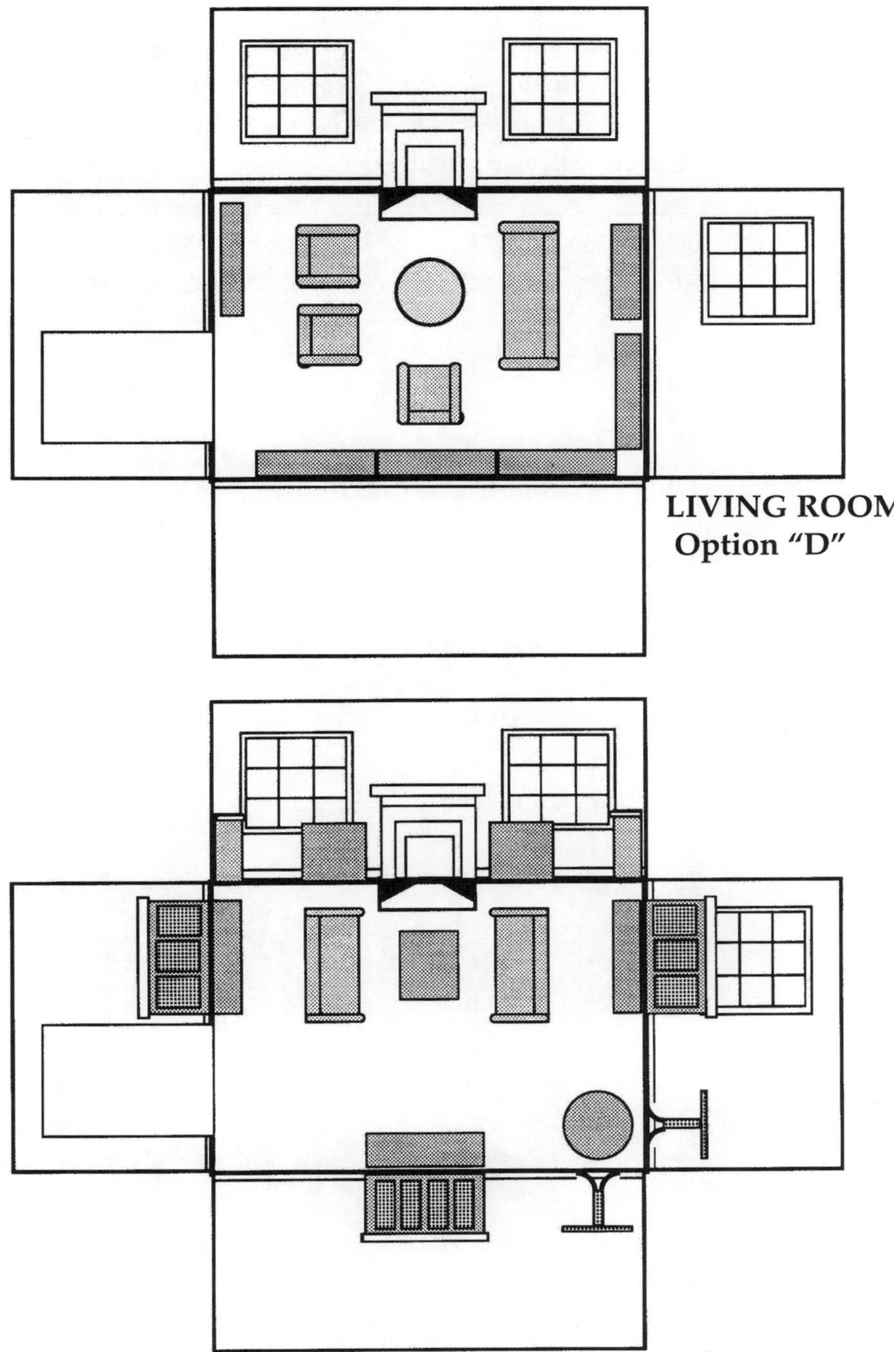

Once you've picked your favorite option, you can draw up a master floor plan. This time sketch in the wall areas to show the height of each piece as well.

Typical Sizes

As a convenience in planning your room layouts, we've listed here some typical sizes for the most commonly used furniture pieces. Clearly, furniture sizes vary widely, so the pieces you already own and ultimately buy will differ to some degree from the sizes shown below. But these will let you get started. Then later you can fine-tune your layouts with your actual sizes.

Sofas	96″ w x 38″ d x 37″ h 84″ w x 38″ d x 37″ h	88″ w x 38″ d x 39″ h 72″ w x 33″ d x 35″ h
Loveseats	74″ w x 38″ d x 37″ h	66″ w x 38″ d x 37″ h
Settees	56″ w x 31″ d x 44″ h	54″ w x 35″ d x 43″ h
Upholstered Chairs	45″ w x 42″ d x 39″ h 36″ w x 34″ d x 36″ h	40″ w x 39″ d x 34″ h 33″ w x 36″ d x 36″ h
Ottomans	33″ w x 22″ d x 17″ h	30″ w x 22″ d x 17″ h
Side Chairs	29″ w x 32″ d x 41″ h	24″ w x 27″ d x 40″ h
Entertainment Centers	48″ w x 25″ d x 64″ h	35″ w x 21″ d x 51″ h
End Tables *	21″ w x 27″ d x 24″ h	20″ w x 26″ d x 23″ h
Coffee Tables *	50″ w x 38″ d x 17″ h 46″ w x 28″ d x 17″ h	50″ w x 34″ d x 18″ h 36″ w x 36″ d x 26″ h
Sofa Tables	57″ w x 17″ d x 30″ h	54″ w x 17″ d x 27″ h
Curio Cabinets	42″ w x 15″ d x 78″ h	36″ w x 17″ d x 81″ h
Dining Tables **	46″ w x 72″ l** x 30″ h 38″ w x 38″ l** x 30″ h	38″ w x 64″ l** x 30″ h ** plus 20″ extension leaves
Dining Chairs	24″ w x 22″ d x 39″ h	18″ w x 21″ d x 38″ h

* Also consider rounds

Buffets	64″ w x 19″ d x 35″ h	60″ w x 16″ d x 32″ h
Hutches	65″ w x 13″ d x 82″ h	57″ w x 14″ d x 50″ h
China Cabinets	62″ w x 16″ d x 83″ h	62″ w x 17″ d x 61″ h
Sideboards	66″ w x 21″ d x 38″ h	62″ w x 19″ d x 35″ h
Desks	72″ w x 35″ d x 30″ h 48″ w x 30″ d x 30″ h	60″ w x 32″ d* x 30″ h
Computer Desks	50″ w x 26″ d x 78″ h	48″ w x 24″ d x 30″ h
File Cabinets	16″ w x 29″ d (letter size) 22″w x 16″ d (side opening)	18″ w x 29″ d (legal size) Heights: 28″ to 56″
Bookcases	Widths: 48″, 40″, 32″	Heights: 73″, 50″, 39″, 28″
Desk Chairs	25″ w x 29″ d x 36″ h	23″ w x 30″ d x 38″ h
Sofa Beds	53″ w x 39″ d x 38″ h (twin) 82″ w x 39″ d x 36″ h (full)	90″ w x 39″ d x 36″d (queen)
Beds	44″ w x 84″ l (twin) 59″ w x 84″ l (full) 66″ w x 89″ l (queen) 82″ w x 89″ l (king) 78″ w x 92″ l (calif. king) 76″ w x 95″ l (calif. king)	41″ w x 84″ l (twin) 57″ w x 86″ l (full) 64″ w x 91″ l (queen) 80″ w x 91″ l (king) (Heights vary from 24″ to 84″)
Night Tables	24″ w x 17″ d x 23″ h	21″ w x 17″ d x 28″ h
Dressers	70″ w x 21″ d x 35″ h 52″ w x 20″ d x 48″ h 42″ w x 19″ d x 31″ h	68″ w x 19″ d x 31″ h 42″ w x 22″ d x 68″ h 36″ w x 19″ d x 51″ h

Armoires	46″ w x 23″ d x 83″ h 43″ w x 21″ d x 78″ h	44″ w x 21″ d x 75″ h

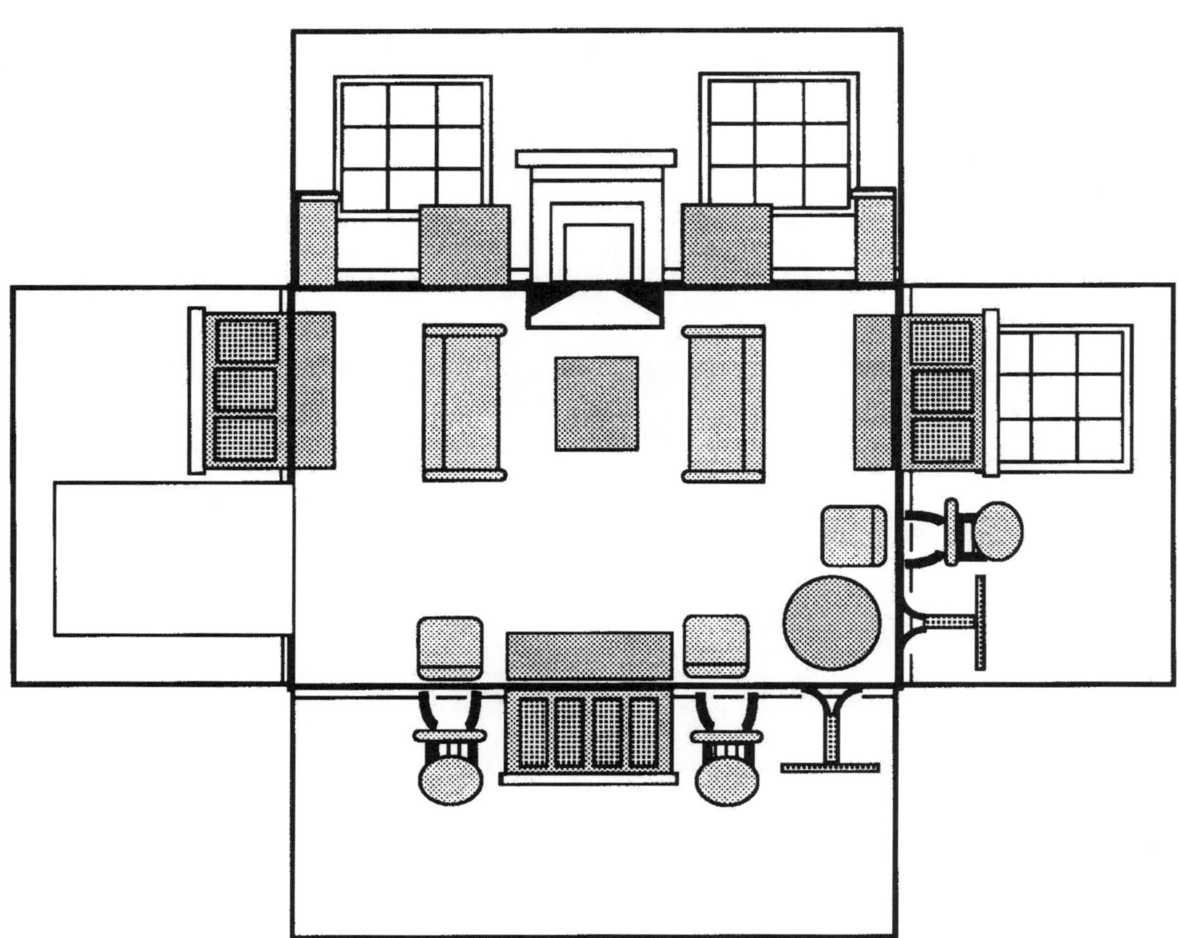

Refining your room plan

Now that you have all the basics in place, give your floor plan one last look. Space permitting, add extra pieces as needed to make the room even more livable.

6. Deciding on the "look" that's right for you

Do you prefer the same basic look for your entire home, or would you like some variety room to room? Either approach can work, although the former will tie things together better. Even so, you may want to make some of your rooms very formal (e.g. living room, dining room, front hall, master bedroom), and the rest more informal (e.g. kitchen, family room, other bedrooms, etc.) Or you might want to make some rooms high-style traditional (e.g. living room and dining room), some country casual (e.g. family room and bedrooms), and others high-tech industrial (e.g. kitchen and laundry room). Or you can make your entire home minimalist post-modern, or Early American, or Victorian, or Baroque European, or country, or '50s modern, or everybody's favorite today—eclectic. Your decision should be based on nothing more than what appeals to you most.

Chances are that many different looks appeal to you, so the problem is deciding which one (or ones) to use. The architectural style of your home may influence your decision, after all it was its "look" that first attracted you to it. But you still have wide latitude. Not only in terms of period and style, but also in terms of emphasis. For example, a few antique pieces and the right accessories are often enough to give an otherwise contemporary room a period shift.

Ultimately, your decision on "look" should be based on the surroundings that will make you the happiest to live in—not on fashion trends or what others say is "in". Think about rooms you've seen and liked, rooms that have somehow appealed to your temperament, your personality and/or your style. Were they period, traditional or modern? Were they urban sophisticated or country cozy? Were they clean and uncluttered or full of interesting things to look at and touch? Were they light and airy or deep and richly textured? Were they feminine, more masculine or somewhere in between?

Did the rooms you liked most capture a particular cultural heritage—American, English, French, Spanish, Italian, Southwestern, Asian, etc.?

Did they suggest a particular time period—17th century, 18th century, 19th century, 20th century, futuristic?

Mull all those things and also think about interiors that you particularly liked in places other than homes—places like hotels and inns, restaurants and clubs, offices and public buildings, historical sites, and even stores.

Don't get hung up on the details at this point. The idea is to run back through your memory to help you visualize the "look" that appeals to you most—overall and then room by room.

7. Deciding how you want each room to "feel"

Even if you decide to give your entire home a consistent "look", you'll want to give each room a special "feel" of its own, not only to reflect its special function, but to add some drama and interest as you move from room to room. Just as a symphony or play would be somewhat monotonous if every movement or scene had the same emotional level or impact, a home or apartment will be a bit monotonous without some emotional variation. You can achieve this variation through your choice of colors, tones, or light levels, by your visual treatments—or through your choice of furnishings and accessories.

Colors, tones, or light levels

You can give some rooms extra drama and special impact by choosing darker colors for your wall and/or floor treatments. Studies, libraries, hallways and powder rooms are all good candidates. Here, deep colors like hunter green, claret and chocolate, or dark wood paneling, or rich-toned wall coverings can all be used to create a dramatic effect.

Working with the same basic color throughout your entire home, you can give some rooms extra interest by using deeper (or lighter) tones. For example, a pale peach in the living room and a 2-shade deeper peach in the dining room. If you prefer a palette of two or three colors (say, for example, yellow, blue and white), you can use one of the colors dominantly in one room and limit the two other colors to trim and accessories. Then in the next room, you can reverse the emphasis.

Light levels can accomplish much the same end. Bathe some rooms with plenty of light, and light others more dramatically with well-placed halogen spotlights, picture lights and opaque shaded table lamps. As you move from lighter to darker to lighter areas, the mood will change even if the basic wall colors are the same. That's because colors take on different hues and tones based on the amount and type of light reflecting off them.

Visual treatment

Another way to add emotional variation is with your choice of fabric patterns and/or wall coverings.

Even using the same basic color palette, you can achieve dramatic transitions room to room. For example, a trellis design wall covering can add a sunny garden effect, a wall covering with a silk or damask finish can add formal elegance, grass cloths or stencil patterns can add informal warmth. Brightly colored floral print fabrics can add gaiety, while subdued floral fabrics can add quiet sophistication. Brocades, chintzes, velvets and tweeds each deliver a different emotional feel, as do the thousands of wallpaper patterns available today.

Choice of furnishings and accessories

Nothing captures a "club feel" as well as leather sofas and easy chairs. Nothing says traditional elegance as well as mahogany. Nothing says modern as well as marble, glass and chrome. Nothing says country as well as stripped pine. Nothing says Asian as well as lacquered cabinets. Nothing says Scandinavian as well as teak. The simple point is that your choice of furniture style and materials will automatically play a dominant role in establishing a room's feel.

But the objects you place on and around your furniture and on your walls and floors, can shift that feel dramatically. For example, let's talk rugs. An oriental, a woven kilim or dhurrie, a solid or patterned broadloom, a sisal carpet, or even bare wood or tiled floors, all will give a room a different feel. Ditto drapery treatments—ranging from elaborate, to simple, or even none at all; and accessories—ranging from few and simple to a room chock full of collectibles. All these contribute to a room's "feel" and are tools you can use.

Decide the basic "feel" you want for each room, and all the specific decisions that follow will be greatly simplified.

8. Fleshing out your rooms plans

If you've followed the suggestions in Chapters 4 and 5, you have a working set of functional drawings which indicate the basic placement of your furniture in each room.

Now you can add to these drawings your decisions on the basic "look" and "feel" that you want for each room (as described in Chapters 6 and 7). Jot them in the margins of your drawings for ongoing reference.

By now, your design plan is beginning to take form. And as you study your functional drawings and take mental tours through each room, you should be able to visualize things in much more detail. The style and character of your furnishing pieces, the overall mood you hope to achieve with accessories, and the general types of fabrics and window treatments should all begin to take shape in your mind. Sketch them in on the four flattened walls surrounding your floor plan.

At this point, you'll probably want to browse through some decorating books, magazines and catalogs to stimulate your visualization. Also, take a tour through a number of furniture and home furnishings stores to see what's available in your price range and to get a feel for actual sizes and how well various pieces work together. This quick tour will also act as a preliminary scouting trip to tell you which stores to visit later when you're ready to buy. You might also want to do some browsing on the Internet. (You'll find a list of web sites worth visiting in the Appendix, starting on page 117.)

As you take more and more mental trips through each room, you'll begin to see the total effect that you want. You can refine your flattened wall drawings a bit further, perhaps indicating where you need pictures, mirrors and other wall hangings, and indicating the type of window treatments.

With this done, it's not too soon to begin compiling your detailed room by room needs lists, using the guides which appear in Part II of this book. You can also add (or confirm) the window treatment you want for each window listed in your Window Measurements tables on pages 15 and 16.

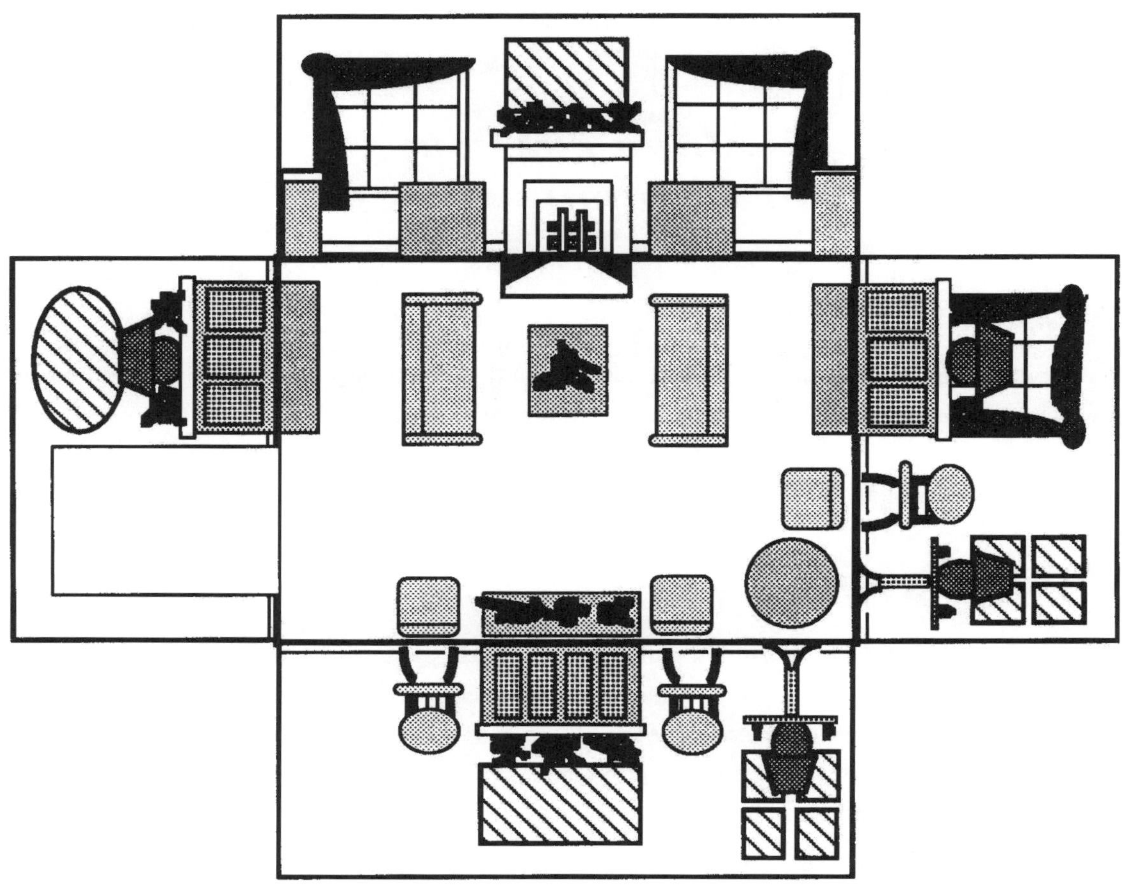

After deciding the "look" and "feel" you want, you can begin to sketch in the wall area detail.

9. Some key early decisions
• color schemes
• lighting
• floor coverings

Now that you've developed your basic room plans, it's time to make some key decisions in these three areas. All of them deserve a bit of extra thought because they'll have a profound impact on the total effect you achieve. Resist just leaping ahead with easy answers like white walls, a bunch of table lamps, and wall-to-wall broadloom carpeting. You might decide to end up with these solutions, but consider other alternatives as well.

1. Color schemes

You know the basic colors you like, for example blue. But that just gives you a starting point. There are thousands of blues to pick from, with subtle and not so subtle differences. And the same is true for every other basic color, including whites and grays. So how do you decide?

There are no hard and fast rules when it comes to color. You can make a room fairly monochromatic or use a range of contrasting or complementary colors, depending on the mood or effect you want to achieve. But a good rule of thumb is to establish a color palette of at least three colors for each room.

The dominant color is the one that you want to have stand out most—even though it might be used principally in your draperies, upholstery and/or carpets. The accent color is the one used in more moderation to add extra richness or excitement, often in trim and accessories. The supporting color is the one that ties everything together, usually in wall coverings and background areas. All that matters is that the colors work well together to create the type of character and personality you want.

Your color palette can be widely spaced and lively—combining colors like white, yellow and blue. Or it can be more closely spaced and subdued—combining colors like mushroom, moss green and persimmon. It can be fairly dark—combining colors like hunter green with tan and rich cherry wood furniture. Or it can be fairly light—combining colors like vanilla, pale peach, and celery.

Obviously, there are a zillion combinations. So how do you pick the color palette that's not only best for each room, but that's also practical to implement in your timetable?

Here's the wrong way to do it:

You've probably read that the professional way to select the colors for a room is to start with a favorite painting or designer carpet that will become the room's focal point, and then use its key colors to define your color palette for the room. Sounds like good advice. But this approach is almost guaranteed to add months, if not years, to your decorating timetable unless you have almost everything custom made. Why? Because your chances of finding good color matches to that favorite painting or carpet at the retail level are practically nil. You'll search and search with little success, as time elapses and frustration grows.

Here's the expedited way to do it:

The best way to select your color palette is to start with an exploratory trip through the housewares, furnishings and linens departments of a few good stores in your area to see what colors the manufacturers are currently featuring. You'll find a great selection of beautifully coordinated colors that you can choose from to define your color palette for each room. And perhaps surprisingly, you'll find these same colors available from a broad range of manufacturers, in just about everything you'll need to furnish your rooms. The reason is that the manufacturers do collaborate to decide what colors to feature each year. And their top designers develop coordinated color palettes to assure that everything works well together.

Rather than start with an arbitrary palette of colors and then try to find things to match them, doesn't it make practical sense to start with a color palette you already know is available, especially when that color palette was created for you by the country's top designers?

In decorating three houses over a six-year period, I became aware of how the home furnishings industry decides what colors to offer and of just how often they change them. At any given time, the stores were full of attractive furnishings and housewares with beautifully coordinated color palettes. Everything worked fabulously well together. But go back to those same stores two years later and you'd find virtually none of those colors still available. A whole new color palette had replaced them. Still great, but entirely different.

When we furnished our first house, rich jeweled-tone colors were everywhere in the stores. Two years later, softer and far more romantic colors had replaced them. Then two years later, warm earthy tones had replaced just about everything again. This was true not just in one store, but in every store we visited. The only exceptions were a few random items that the retailers had not been able to sell the previous season.

We wondered how all these independent manufacturers of home furnishings agreed on what to make next year's colors, and how they actually coordinated all their efforts? The answer was that most all of them rely on an organization called The Color Marketing Group.

The Color Marketing Group is made up of more than 1,500 design professionals from various industries, the very people whose job it is to select colors for their companies' products. As a group they debate and then forecast general color trends, and then, as they define it, —"translate these general trends into salable colors." The majority of the colors we see in the marketplace today are the result of the forecasts done by the CMG several years ago.

Every year, the CMG gives its members a palette of specific colors to use in their products two years from now. These colors are rarely simple, straightforward colors like tan, green and black; rather they're complex blends of several colors, creating a family of tones and hues that are both distinctive and highly compatible. They have enticing names and poetic descriptions as in the examples listed below. And for each, color swatches and pigment formulas are provided to the manufacturers.

Here are the Consumer colors for this year, exactly as The Color Marketing Group describes them:

Wild Berry: A pure, newly true, bright red. Religious iconography and the two thousandth anniversary of the birth of Christ may be causing new interest in true red.

Innocent Blush: A sheer pink that envelops the viewer in softness and comfort. Feminine and nurturing, slight peach undertones.

Red Rock: An Australian-influenced metallic color that will generate a reintroduction of iron ore tones.

Biscotti: A new neutral that is softer than the traditional camel.

Spaqua: The green side of water imagery. However, it is best to think of this hue as the edge color of a thick sheet of plate glass. Spaqua is playful and versatile.

Wasabi: A nature-inspired hue from Asia, where foliage is more yellow than in North America and Europe. This sophisticated hue is a sheer wash of celadon, faintly yellowed, with a whisper of gray. Truly chameleon.

Aero Blue: This hue is considered timeless and spiritual. Envision a sky approaching dusk. It also evokes memories of historical paint and wall covering colors.

Atlantis Blue: A universal blue for all cultures, Atlantis is intense and iridescent. The slight influence of green adds a unique spark that subtly stirs the psyche.

Royal Plum: Spirituality and ceremonial ritual inspired this hue. Royal Plum is a color icon of royalty and wealth. This hue can serve as a neutral, a bridge to other colors or stand alone.

White Veil: Speaks of the growing importance of white, with the special caveat that whites will not be white. Translucency, layering and novel coating technologies will push white into new tinted directions creating chameleon appearances.

Aluminum Foil: Pure metal continues to interest many designers as a stand alone product element, or juxtaposed against other materials. The coldest, most urban interpretation of silver.

Colorado Mist: Metallic or pearlized, this sophisticated neutral bridges beige and gray. It is described as a warm silver that is both Zen and urban.

And here are the Contract/Commercial colors for this year, exactly as The Color Marketing Group describes them:

Bay Fog: A complex neutral that evokes impressions of gray, blue and purple.

Chakura Purple: A veiled, mystical lavender. It is red-based and midtone. Excellent as a foil for other colors in the palette.

Copper Leaf: Copper that is less harsh than the color of a new penny, with more depth and texture, and a hint of muted luster.

Fiesta: A new direction for orange—it is more refined and sophisticated for upscale markets as blue influences it away from the harsh and brash orange of the past.

Frosted Jade: This beautiful, dreamy gray-green, reminiscent of Chinese porcelain, in a new direction for neutral.

Hematite: Neither warm nor cool, this deep, dark, grayed purple is a replacement for black, softer and more amiable.

Meritage: Just like several wines combine to make a fine vintage, Meritage is a complex brown-influenced purple.

Salsa Lito: Originating from Asian lacquer, the browned red is strong and opulent.

Silkworm: Creamy, light tan neutral, warm and comfortable. Works and plays well with other colors.

Silver Streak: A warm, mercurial silver with a soft sheen. Silver Streak was created for this palette using a full pearlescent pigment base without any metallic content.

Spa: Water-influenced blue moves away from greens and teal. This is a pure color that is healing and healthful.

Squid Ink: A dark gray-influenced blue. Calm and serene like a starless sky at midnight.

Thai Gold: A rich, yellow gold reemerges from the ancient Far East.

Tip Taupe: A mixer color that sneaks up on you from several directions. A beautiful neutral that quietly adds a new dimension to taupe with a crisper, less muted appearance.

While some of these names may sound pretty wild and conjure up an image of a riot of color, in actuality they're far more subtle and compatible. And, of course, each manufacturer will rename them to reflect their own image but the color formulas will be basically the same.

These lists are included to give you some idea of the complexity of the colors that you'll find in the stores in any given year, and to underscore the near impossibility of finding precise color matches to the colors in that favorite painting or designer carpet that the decorators tell you to use for your color palette.

So start with what's actually available at retail. From it, select the color palette you like best when you see it. Then purchase an array of small items like washcloths or coffee mugs to use as your color chips for further planning. Getting a great color look is just that easy! (Incidentally, you can visit The Color Marketing Group's web site to see what colors they're planning for next year by connecting to www.colormarketing.org.)

2. Lighting

On a copy of your flattened floor plans, make a preliminary indication of where you'll need table and floor lamps. If the room has wall and/or overhead lights (sconces, chandeliers, recessed spots, track lights, etc.) sketch them in too. But don't stop there. The object is not just to light the room, but to use lighting to give the entire space the extra drama and special mood that you'd like.

Think about how lighting is used in the theater. You almost never see the entire stage lit to the same uniform light level. That tends to flatten out everything. Instead, pools of light contrast against areas of relative darkness. Spotlights rivet your attention on the star performer. Lights of different intensity come from different directions, providing definition and depth through the use of soft and strong shadows.

Good lighting creates contrasts. As in photography and painting, it's the interplay of light and darkness that makes the scene truly come alive.

Also, consider the impact of light and darkness on colored surfaces. Because the color we see is really reflected light, a room that's creatively lit transforms an otherwise solid color mass into a full range of beautifully harmonious hues and tones that add richness, character and depth. A beige wall appears almost off-white where full intensity light strikes it, displays a subtle range of warm beiges and tans in areas that are less brightly lit, and appears dark taupe in the full shadow areas. But if the light in the room was flat and uniform, all you'd see on the walls is a fairly boring mass of beige.

With all this in mind, go back to your flattened floor plan and sketch in your final lighting plan considering not just where the lamps go but where you want the light to fall. To help you visualize this, you may want to use a tracing paper overlay and draw in "light circles" that indicate the effects of lights of various intensities.

Some useful lighting techniques to consider:

- Picture lights—either small spots in the ceiling, or tube lights extending from the frame tops.

- Cabinet lights—with halogen lights illuminating the interiors of glass-fronted display cabinets, or mounted under wall-hung cabinets.

- Bookcase lights—using small strip lights mounted vertically on the risers to illuminate all the shelves.

All these techniques will add points of interest and cast soft light into the room.

Your lighting effect will almost always be more dramatic if you don't see the glare of your bulbs head on. To mask them, while also achieving good general illumination, you'll probably use translucent lampshades. But consider how darker opaque shades concentrate all the light downward, with just a soft glow on the ceiling above. Their effect is, at the same time, both more subtle and more dramatic.

Remember, you can change the room's mood through the use of wall and table lamp dimmers. They're inexpensive and easy to install. Consider them especially for your wall sconces, recessed spots, and hanging lights.

Once you've fine-tuned your lighting plans, draw up a final list of lamp types, sizes and styles for each room on the Planning Guide lists in Part II of this book. And don't forget related supplies like extension cords, multi-plug blocks, dimmers and light bulbs (including spares).

3. Floor coverings

Except in kitchens and baths, wall-to-wall carpeting is the most common floor covering used today; and it's perhaps the least expensive. But don't make a snap decision to use it before considering all your alternatives. Floors represent a large mass of color and texture that greatly impacts the feel of a room. And you have a great many options:

- Wood floors with decorative area rugs. If your wood floors need refinishing anyway, you can choose to have them stained darker or left natural. You can even stain them with transparent colors, or have them stained (using masking tape or stencils) in a range of wood tones to create classic faux parquet effects. And if a wood floor is really beat up, you can paint and antique it in one or more colors and patterns to give it a country period look.

- If you'd like wood floors but don't have them, you can install prefinished wood parquet tiles or use one of the new laminate floating floors that look like fine wood flooring and resist wear, water and staining. This makes them suitable even in high abuse areas like family rooms, kitchens, baths, exercise rooms, mud rooms and foyers.

- Ceramic tiles can give you the look of terra-cotta tile, stone, brick or marble. And they can be installed square-on or at a diagonal. You can also use rectangular tiles to create patterns like herringbones, running bonds, basket weaves, etc. And decorative tiles can be used with them as inserts, or to create center features and borders.

- Resilient vinyl flooring need not be limited to kitchens, laundries and bathrooms. Some higher-end vinyls do a remarkable job of approximating natural materials like stone, brick, marble, tile, wood, etc. in both color and texture. And you'll find unique patterns and designs available only in vinyl.

- If you do decide on wall-to-wall carpeting, consider textures as an alternative to standard plush broadlooms. Berbers, sisals, twists, and carved patterns are all available. And then there are solids, multicolors and patterns to select from. Each will give your room a different feel.

In making your final decisions on floor coverings, remember that it's the floor treatment as much as anything else that pulls all the many elements in the room together. A neutral-colored broadloom carpet will probably do the job nicely. But you can go much further if you open up your imagination.

10. Paint: the quickest, easiest, least expensive way to transform that empty box into a beautiful room

Even in a great house or apartment, there's usually a room or two devoid of any architectural interest. In fact, there may be problems with poorly placed windows, doors, beams, built-ins, etc. Better to deal with and resolve these problems first, before sailing into the rest of your room decorating.

Short of expensive remodeling, the best way to minimize, and in fact capitalize upon these problems, is with decorative painting. It's also by far your fastest and least expensive solution.

Consider these few analogies:

- There's nothing plainer than a blank white artist's canvas. Yet with paint alone, that canvas can be turned into a masterpiece.
- A fashion model, a showgirl or a movie actress can often look very plain without her make-up. It's not uncommon to find that her eyes are a bit too small, her nose a bit too thick, her lips a bit too thin, her complexion sallow or splotchy. In short, nothing special to look at. Yet with make-up alone, that model can be transformed into a dazzling beauty.
- Stage scenery before painting is usually just framed canvas flats hooked together, two dimensional cut-out shapes, and plain canvas backdrops. Yet with paint alone, they can be transformed into convincingly real building interiors, exteriors, and landscapes. So for those "problem rooms," go back to your plain flattened room drawings. Ask yourself what each room lacks or has wrong with it? Then consider how to correct it, or minimize it, with decorative painting.

For example, the far wall may be devoid of absolutely any interest—just a big, solid, blank wall. With paint alone, you can transform that wall into the room's richest element. It can become a wall of smooth limestone blocks, a wall of marble or wood panels, or a wall of richly aged Tuscan stucco. It's all done with paint.

You may find one or more walls with windows so tightly jammed into the corners that side draperies are impossible. With paint in contrasting colors, you can articulate portions of the window trim moldings to coordinate with a fabric-covered boxed cornice or valance at the top of the window. This will give your windows a fully finished, integrated look, without draperies. You can use the same technique to integrate your doorways, baseboards and ceiling moldings.

You may have a fairly drab fireplace. With paint you can turn it into a marbleized showpiece, perhaps with different types and colors of faux marble to accent its key features. It's all done with paint, and it's far easier than you might think.

Bookcases, built-ins, columns, beams and soffits can all be given distinctive treatments. Again, it's all done with paint.

Stenciled borders at wall tops or at chair rail height, around windows and doors, or in larger form to create headboards, etc., are other possibilities.

Decorative painting can be used to give otherwise beat-up chairs, tables, dressers and cabinets handsome new life. Again with just paint.

Going further, you can add wooden moldings and/or chair rails and ceiling medallions to a room and then articulate them with paint. And you can, of course, also use wallpaper panels and borders and even wallpaper murals, if you want that effect. For an especially long room, you might also consider installing a freestanding room divider that's decorated as if it were a wall.

A word about decorative painting:

This catchall title includes everything from the decorative use of straight solid colors, to antiquing, to faux finishing, to trompe l'oeil. There are a large number of great books available today showing you what's possible and exactly how to do it. Even if you decide to hire a painter to do your decorative painting for you, it's worth looking through these books to get ideas and to show your painter the effect you want.

I think you'll be amazed at how simple most of the techniques are (which is why we chose to do our own decorative painting after hiring a professional painter to do all the prep and base coats for us). Only advanced trompe l'oeil work and hand-painted murals may require the expertise of an artist. Most everything else can be done with rollers, brushes, sponges and rags.

Here's the basic concept:

- You paint the whole area with a solid mid-range color.

- After it dries, you sponge on or rag on a lighter-colored glaze, which is nothing more than a lighter color paint mixed 50/50 with a transparent glaze material. Most any paint store will have transparent glazes available.

- When that dries, you sponge or rag on a darker-colored glaze, which again, is just paint mixed 50/50 with a transparent glaze material.

- If you want, you can add veining with a small brush (or feather) dipped in thinned paint of a darker or lighter color. Using masking tape to guide you, quickly add grout lines with full-bodied paint.

- The whole process goes surprisingly fast, and you can preview the effect of each step by sponging or ragging on each glaze, in turn, onto a test board before adding the glaze to the wall. If, in your preview you think a glaze should be lighter or darker, just add a little lighter or darker paint. And any mistakes on the wall can be quickly corrected by sponging on additional coats of lighter or darker glaze in the problem areas. You can even give yourself a fresh start by covering up part of the glazed area with more of the base coat.

- An almost foolproof way to pick your three basic colors for the base coat and the two glazes is to select an appropriate paint strip from the color chip display at your paint store. On the same strip, pick every other color with the middle one for your wall base color and the other two for your lighter and darker glazes. You'll need about four times as much of the middle color as you will for the other two. For all three, a satin finish latex paint is recommended because it's the easiest to use.

If all this sounds like more than you want to handle, just hire a good painter. But the point is that you can transform an otherwise blah or problem room space into a gem, through the use of decorative painting.

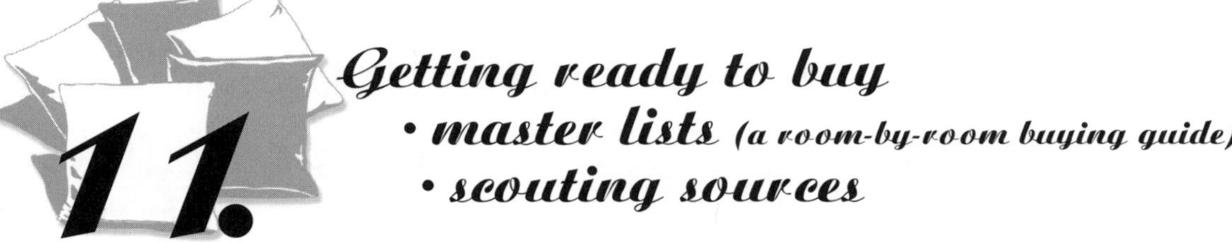

11. Getting ready to buy
• master lists (a room-by-room buying guide)
• scouting sources

Now that you've completed your design plans, it's time to finalize your needs lists, using the Planning Guides contained in Part II. You'll find a detailed explanation of how to use them at the start of that section. The basic idea is this:

- For each room, detail all your needs, including the things you already have and the new items you'll have to buy. (Later this will serve as your inventory list for each room.)

- Using these lists, summarize things-to-buy by category (e.g. furniture, lighting, etc.) These category lists become your shopping lists because they summarize your needs the same way that the stores group their merchandise. As such, they help you shop more efficiently and economically.

Before you begin the actual buying process, you should first scout out and rank your potential sources for each type of merchandise. Here you're just taking a quick walk through each store to see if you like what they carry, to gauge the breadth of their line, and to assess their general price ranges. You can scout a large number of stores in a single day if you don't get sidetracked doing actual shopping or stopping to talk with the salespeople. And don't forget to include furniture warehouse outlets in the stores you visit.

After visiting each store, make a few notes to aid your recollection later. Your goal now is just to learn which stores to start with when it comes time to begin buying.

Another way to scout potential sources is to quickly scan all those store catalogs that come in the mail and that you find inserted in your newspapers. While these catalogs are usually tied into specific sales, they'll give you a pretty good idea of each store's quality, style of merchandise, and their price range.

Catalogs from mail order sources should also be scanned and saved, if you like what you see. Specialized mail order companies can be a great source for items like linens, curtains, decorative accessories, and porch and deck furniture. You can expand the number of mail order catalogs you scan by calling some of the companies advertising in the back of home magazines. Also check out their web sites.

There are also growing numbers of great specialized web sites designed to help you plan, select and buy everything you need to decorate your home. Spend a few evenings window shopping on line. It's an amazing source, especially for special and unusual items that you might not find locally. You'll be able to browse quickly through the collections of thousands of manufacturers and home furnishings dealers. And you can buy direct from individuals and antique dealers through auction sites like e-Bay, often finding great bargains. A list of some of the more productive Internet web sites appears in the Appendix.

At the end of this step, you're totally organized to shop efficiently. You know precisely what you need and where to go to find most of it.

12. Buying like a pro · what the furniture stores don't tell you

Because furniture is the largest expense item and because typically it takes the longest lead-time for delivery, let's start there.

How can you complete your project quickly, when it takes an average of 12 to 16 weeks for a typical store to deliver its furniture orders?

The answer, of course, is to persuade them to deliver it to you in 2 to 3 weeks. It's possible far more often than you might think.

Those 12 to 16 week delivery schedules assume that the store has no inventory, that the manufacturer has no inventory, that the manufacturer will sit on your order until they can group it with several others for a more efficient run, and that they'll even delay shipping it until they can combine your order with others going to the same area. The actual manufacturing time is really just a few days, and shipping takes just a few days more. All the rest of the time is just wait time.

To eliminate this long delay, start with—don't end with—your critical timing needs when you talk with the store manager or salesperson. Tell them, "I'm decorating a property and need all my furniture pieces within 3 weeks to meet my completion schedule." If they think you're talking about a commercial property, so much the better, because then they'll take your need for speed very seriously. Also, they'll see their ability to meet it as the difference between getting or losing your order. And it's a big order because you're talking about buying several pieces at the same time.

Thus motivated, a good store will suggest several alternatives. First, they'll show you their floor samples available for immediate delivery. (If they're a chain, they'll call their other stores, too, to determine what's available.) Then they'll check their main warehouse for inventory. (Many stores keep a reserve of several pieces to fill the emergency needs of their commercial customers.)

Then they'll call their manufacturers to determine what they already have in inventory, and what they're planning to run within the next week. If asked, they will also show you the furniture styles and fabrics specified for orders placed several weeks ago. Then they'll call the manufacturer to see if there's still time to hitchhike your order onto the next run. If there is, they may even be able to let you pick a different fabric.

Of course, all these alternatives do limit your choice to what's available. But even so, chances are good you'll find a great solution to your needs. Maybe not everything at the first store, but it's far more likely when you use this approach at your top three store picks.

If you have your heart set on a unique fabric for one or more pieces, consider using a custom upholsterer. Many of New York's high-end stores routinely order pieces covered in muslin and ship them to a custom upholsterer for completion in fabrics and trim specified by the customer's interior designer. You can use this approach yourself—ordering new furniture covered in muslin, or inexpensive floor samples with fabric damage, or used furniture you buy or already have. A custom upholsterer should be able to re-cover them for you in two to three weeks. They'll have wonderful fabric samples to pick from. Or you can buy your own fabric at an outlet or showroom, once your upholsterer tells you how much will be needed.

In buying the wooden furniture for the houses we decorated, we used all these approaches plus several more. Estate sales, auctions and antique stores for period pieces (just 5 or 10 minutes at each stop can tell you if they have what you want.) A local craftsman built us custom shaker-style cabinets, tables and headboards. (We alerted him beforehand to reserve time for our order, contingent on the house closings going as planned.) We even used catalog showrooms representing North Carolina furniture manufacturers. All this may sound like a lot of effort, but added together it took us only about three days of shopping to have all our furniture ordered.

After your furniture orders are placed, you can move on to all the other items you'll need. And this will go even faster because the stores will have most all of it in stock. And at this point, you'll know exactly what fabrics you've chosen for your upholstered pieces, making final color decisions on carpeting, draperies and accessories easier as well.

Here's how to save time and money buying those hundreds of items still on your lists. As an example, let's start with your lighting needs list to see how it works:

The best way to buy lamps is to walk into a pre-selected lamp store (or lamp department) with your clipboard and tape measure. Go directly to the store manager or senior person saying, "I'm furnishing a property and need 25 lamps. What kind of discount will apply?" After the manager stops salivating over the potential size of your order, she will drop everything to personally show you the lamps that come closest to your particular style/price/color/size needs. You'll save an enormous amount of time because she knows her merchandise far better than you ever will, and she'll often bring out items from the back room or show you items in her supplier catalogs that she can get within a few days. Within a few minutes, you'll know if this store is the right place for you to buy. And if you decide "yes," you can have her write up the order and then give her an extra day to box up all your lamps for pick up the subsequent day. Why wait around, when you could be off to the bedding store to repeat the same process for your linens and blankets?

To make the above approach practical, you need both your compiled Category Lists (pages 100-114) and your Room-by-Room Lists (pages 56-97) with their more detailed size/color/style specs. Make photocopies of these compiled lists and put them into your clipboard, along with photocopies of your flattened room plans. (You can also insert color chips, fabric swatches, etc. if you'd like.) Using photocopies is a good idea because you can then write notes on them without messing up your masters. Using a clipboard also sends a silent signal that you're a serious, volume buyer.

As you acquire items, cross them off your Category Lists and check off the "HAVE" boxes in your Room-by-Room Lists. If necessary, update the final specs for size, color and style if they'll influence your decisions on items yet to be purchased. It's also a good practice to update the final specs on all the items listed on your Room-by-Room Lists, then you'll have a final record of exactly what went into each room.

As mentioned earlier, there's a real feeling of accomplishment as you see the number of items on your "needs list" melt away. Before long, you'll be down to a handful of items left to buy.

Not surprisingly, it's these last few items that will be the most difficult and time consuming to find. For some reason, none of the stores you've visited had them—at least not in the style, size or color you wanted. That's a good tip-off that they're not in general distribution. This leaves you with three alternatives:

1. Expand your search to boutiques and specialty stores. (Call first.)

2. Use mail order sources. (Via catalogs or the Internet.)

3. Reassess your needs. (The item you want may no longer be available. Ask yourself what would work just as well? Facing the realities, a substitution may be the smart move.)

It's important to keep in mind the two underlying principles in becoming a successful and time-efficient decorator:

1. You'll always achieve the best results if you clearly separate the creative design phase from the buying phase. You do the creative design phase first, on paper, thoughtfully and quietly at home. Then, only when you have completed your master plans and needs lists, tackle the buying phase—doing so aggressively, like a professional buyer. By separating the two phases, you save yourself an enormous amount of frustration, confusion and time—not to mention expense.

2. While some decision flexibility is needed to complete your project on time, you should never allow yourself to cross the line into compromising your design concept. Don't settle on an item that doesn't really excite you just to complete your list. If you've been realistic in your design plans and have developed your color palette as described in Chapter 9, you'll find just about everything you need is out there. You may choose to make substitutions if availability and price dictate. And you may see items in the stores that excite you even more than your original plans. Go for them, but only if they're true to your overall design concept.

13. Putting it all together

If you're amassing all your purchases for a single move-in date, as we did, here are a few tips that might prove useful:

- On a separate photocopy set of our Room-by-Room Lists, we used a highlighter to cross off each item as we added it to our inventory.
- From a moving company, we bought a number of large cartons to consolidate floppy items like linens, small loose items like kitchen gadgets, and unboxed items like pictures and wall hangings. We also bought smaller boxes, bubble wrap and tape to protect fragile items like silk flower arrangements, vases, etc. All these we prepackaged before sticking them in our garage.
- On every carton added to our inventory, we wrote the final room destination in bold marker—along with a brief description of the carton's contents, unless it was obvious from its labeling.
- This let us pack things tightly into storage without the need to keep rehandling it.
- On the appointed move day, we rented a truck and about a dozen padded moving blankets. We hired a local moving crew to load the truck for us. They did all the heavy lifting. Based on their experience, they loaded the truck far more efficiently than we could have done. Which means they fit everything in, as well as packed and stacked it to preclude shifting and breakage.
- At the receiving end, we hired a crew to unload everything for us. We posted signs at the entrance to each room so they could put everything where we wanted it. For the heavy furniture, we told them where to place it, consulting our flattened room drawings as necessary to aid our memory.
- We hired one of the unloading crew for the next two to three days to assist us with unpacking and setup. This let us concentrate on the creative stuff, while he assembled beds, installed drapery

hardware, put china and glassware into their cabinets, hooked up the stereo, etc. An extra pair of hands and a strong back also proved invaluable in fine-tuning furniture placement. It was also nice to have someone take over the chore of getting rid of all the packaging materials.

- The few items we scheduled for local delivery, like major appliances and mattresses, we had delivered on the first day after the move in. The delivery crew placed them for us. Appliance hook-up was scheduled for later that same day.

- For the first house, we tried living amid all the chaos. That was OK, but we decided to eat and sleep off-site for our subsequent projects. There's nothing like retreating to a comfortable, fully equipped place with TV, a hot shower and plenty of towels to restore your energy and spirits for the next long day ahead. Above all, you don't want your enthusiasm to fade. And that can happen, if you allow yourself to get over tired.

- Typically, we worked 8 to 10 hours a day on our decorating and set-up. More than that and you may start to slow down. So we locked up, went out to dinner, and relaxed for the rest of the evening.

- Handled this way, we were able to fully furnish and fully accessorize a large four-bedroom house by the end of the fourth day after move in.

If your move is local, an alternative is to receive all your major deliveries at the new place and use it as the site for your inventory storage. You won't need to consolidate and box your purchases. Just deposit them there in their original store bags and boxes, preferably placed in the rooms they'll be used in. You can also have all your big appliances installed before move in.

You'll still need an official move-in date, to transfer all your current possessions. You'll probably want to hire a local mover to do this for you. You can follow the same procedure that we used. Hire someone for two to three days to help with the setup. Pace yourself so that marathon work doesn't kill your enthusiasm. Get away every night for a hot shower, a relaxing meal, a little TV and a comfortable bed to sleep in. Within a few days, you'll really be ready to move into your beautifully completed new home or apartment.

14. The "wrap party"

If you've watched *This Old House* on public TV, you know that they end each project with a "wrap party." It's a way to celebrate the project's successful completion, while giving everyone who contributed a sincere "thank you," along with the chance to see the project's final outcome. Everyone loves a party!

There's another, perhaps more important reason that they hold a wrap party. By setting its date far in advance, they're firmly committing to a target complete date. That gives sharper focus to all their efforts, each and every day throughout the project.

Consider how deadlines mobilize our energies, bring out our famed American ingenuity to the fullest, prompt us to make decisive decisions, and add to the persuasive clout of the project team leader. "Opening Night!" "D-Day" "April 15th" "X Shopping Days to Christmas!" All these fixed target dates force us to accomplish things in a time frame that we might have thought impossible. And certainly without these fixed deadlines, many of us would keep procrastinating and making excuses forever!

Recognizing this, we decided to schedule wrap parties for all our projects. A few weeks before our planned move-in date, we sent out invitations to everyone involved in the project. This included our realtor, attorney, tradespeople, and helpers, along with their spouses. They all greatly appreciated the invitation because they rarely get to see the final results of their efforts. Also, it allowed them to show off all their hard work to their spouses. An added bonus was a higher level of camaraderie with each of them, giving us a great team of new friends we could call upon in the future.

So do consider scheduling your own wrap party. (Should an unforeseen setback occur, you can always postpone it until later. But don't admit that to anyone!)

After the wrap party is over and you've relaxed a few days in your beautiful new home, send out more invitations to family and friends for the official housewarming party. Tell them not to bring gifts, because you already have everything you need based on your fabulous planning.

Great success on your project!

PART II

Planning Guides

Planning Guides

How to use them to save time and buy like a pro:

On the following pages, you'll find structured buying lists to help you pre-plan, organize and speed up the acquisition of those hundreds of items needed to completely furnish your home.

First of all, they'll help you remember dozens of items you might initially forget. And second, and far more important, with these lists you'll become an efficient professional buyer, deserving the personal assistance of store management—rather than just an ignored retail shopper searching for hours through stacks of merchandise and standing in long checkout lines.

Here's how to use the guides:

Section I
This is your room-by-room buying guide (living room, dining room, master bedroom, etc.). Start here.

Step #1 — For each room you plan to decorate, first indicate the Dominant Color(s) you've chosen for that room. (There's space for this right above the lists.) Then simply check off all the items that you want or need (using the NEED box). If you already have an item that you want or need in that room, check-off both the NEED and HAVE boxes. This way you'll have a complete list of everything that will finally go into that room. You'll find that most of the items you'll need for each room are already listed for you (sofa, love seat, coffee table, etc.). Plus there are extra lines so that you can add any other items you may need.

Step #2 — For each of the items you've checked, specify the quantity you'll need for that room (end tables-2), the preferred size (18" x 24"), the color (natural pine), and the style (country).

After you've completed the lists in Section I, move on to Section II.

Section II

This section allows you to group all the items you've specified in Section I by "category" (furniture, lighting, etc.) *But in Section II, you should list only those items that you still need to purchase.* Section II lets you summarize your shopping lists in the same way that stores group their merchandise. As such, these Category Lists will help you to shop more efficiently and economically.

Step #3 — After you've completed the two steps in Section I, simply use that same data to make up your shopping lists in Section II. Indicate the total number of each item still needed for all your rooms, along with the appropriate Room Codes. This will facilitate referring back to the more detailed size/color/style specs in your Section I lists. (For example: Table Lamps. . . 18, Room Codes. . . A, C, D, G, I, J, K, L,). For your convenience, a list of Room Codes appears at the bottom of each Section II page.

Using your lists while shopping

As described in chapter 12 on page 44, the best way to buy lamps is to walk into a pre-scouted lamp store (or lamp department) with your clipboard and tape measure. Go directly to the store manager or senior person, saying—"I'm furnishing a property and I need 28 lamps. What kind of discount will apply?" After the manager stops salivating over the potential size of your order, she'll drop everything to personally show you the lamps that come closest to your style/price/color/size needs. You'll save an enormous amount of time because she knows her merchandise far better than you ever will, and she'll often bring out items from the back room or show you items in her catalogs that she can get within a few days. Within a very few minutes, you'll know if the store is the right place for you to buy. And if you decide "yes", you can have her write up the order and then give her an extra day to box up all your lamps for pick-up the subsequent day. Why wait around, when you could be off to the bedding store to repeat the same process for your linens and blankets?

To make the above approach practical, you need both your compiled Section II "Category" Lists *and* your Section I "Room-by-Room" Lists with their more detailed size/color/style specs. Just make photocopies of these compiled lists and put them into your clipboard, along with photocopies of your "flattened" floor plans. (You can also insert color chips, fabric swatches, etc. if you'd like.) Using photocopies is a good idea, because you can then write notes on them without messing up your masters. Using a clipboard also sends a silent signal to the store manager that you're a serious, volume buyer.

Keeping your master lists up to date

As you acquire each item, cross it off in Section II and check-off the "HAVE" box in Section I. If necessary, update the final specs for size, color and style if they'll influence your decisions on items yet to be purchased. It's also a good practice to eventually update to your final specs all the items in Section I, because then you'll have a final record of exactly what went into each room.

Planning Guides

Section I

Detailed By Room

PLANNING GUIDES — DETAILED BY ROOM

A. Living Room

Dominant Color(s): ______________________

Need	Have	Item	#	Size	Color	Style
Furniture:						
❑	❑	Sofas	____	____________	____________	______________
❑	❑	Love seats	____	____________	____________	______________
❑	❑	Upholstered chairs	____	____________	____________	______________
❑	❑	Ottomans	____	____________	____________	______________
❑	❑	Side chairs	____	____________	____________	______________
❑	❑	Coffee tables	____	____________	____________	______________
❑	❑	End tables	____	____________	____________	______________
❑	❑	Sofa back tables	____	____________	____________	______________
❑	❑	Lamp tables	____	____________	____________	______________
❑	❑	TV cabinet/stand	____	____________	____________	______________
❑	❑	Bookcases	____	____________	____________	______________
❑	❑	Shelf units	____	____________	____________	______________
❑	❑	Display cabinets	____	____________	____________	______________
❑	❑	Storage cabinets	____	____________	____________	______________
❑	❑	Desk	____	____________	____________	______________
❑	❑	Desk chair	____	____________	____________	______________
❑	❑	Bench	____	____________	____________	______________
❑	❑	Audio cabinet	____	____________	____________	______________
❑	❑	____________	____	____________	____________	______________
❑	❑	____________	____	____________	____________	______________
❑	❑	____________	____	____________	____________	______________
Lighting:						
❑	❑	Table lamps	____	____________	____________	______________
❑	❑	Floor lamps	____	____________	____________	______________
❑	❑	Wall lamps	____	____________	____________	______________
❑	❑	Ceiling lamps	____	____________	____________	______________
❑	❑	____________	____	____________	____________	______________
❑	❑	____________	____	____________	____________	______________

A. Living Room (cont.)

Need	Have	Item	#	Size	Color	Style
❑	❑	Picture lamps	____	____________	____________	________________
❑	❑	Desk lamp	____	____________	____________	________________
❑	❑	______________	____	____________	____________	________________
❑	❑	______________	____	____________	____________	________________
❑	❑	______________	____	____________	____________	________________
Flooring:						
❑	❑	Carpets	____	____________	____________	________________
❑	❑	Area rugs	____	____________	____________	________________
❑	❑	Tile/sheet goods	____	____________	____________	________________
❑	❑	______________	____	____________	____________	________________
❑	❑	______________	____	____________	____________	________________
Windows:						
❑	❑	Drapes/valances	____	____________*	____________	________________
❑	❑	Curtains	____	____________*	____________	________________
❑	❑	Blinds/shades	____	____________*	____________	________________
❑	❑	Drape/curtain rods	____	____________*	____________	________________
❑	❑	______________	____	____________	____________	________________
❑	❑	______________	____	____________	____________	________________
Electronics:						
❑	❑	Television set	____	____________	____________	________________
❑	❑	VCR	____	____________	____________	________________
❑	❑	Audio system	____	____________	____________	________________
❑	❑	Telephone	____	____________	____________	________________
❑	❑	______________	____	____________	____________	________________
Other:						
❑	❑	______________	____	____________	____________	________________
❑	❑	______________	____	____________	____________	________________
❑	❑	______________	____	____________	____________	________________
❑	❑	______________	____	____________	____________	________________
❑	❑	______________	____	____________	____________	________________

* See pages 15 and 16 for precise sizes

A. Living Room (cont.)

Need	Have	Item	#	Size of Area	Color Scheme	Style/ Motif
Accessories:						
		Wall hangings —				
❑	❑	Over mantle	____	____	____	____
❑	❑	Over couch	____	____	____	____
❑	❑	Above cabinet	____	____	____	____
❑	❑	Wall area "A"	____	____	____	____
❑	❑	Wall area "B"	____	____	____	____
❑	❑	Wall area "C	____	____	____	____
❑	❑	Wall area "D"	____	____	____	____
❑	❑	Wall area "E"	____	____	____	____
❑	❑	Mirrors	____	____	____	____
❑	❑	Pictures	____	____	____	____
❑	❑	Clock	____	____	____	____
❑	❑	Plaques	____	____	____	____
❑	❑	____	____	____	____	____
❑	❑	____	____	____	____	____
		Tabletop items —				
❑	❑	Mantle top	____	____	____	____
❑	❑	Coffee table top	____	____	____	____
❑	❑	End table tops	____	____	____	____
❑	❑	Sofa table top	____	____	____	____
❑	❑	Cabinet tops	____	____	____	____
❑	❑	Desk accessories	____	____	____	____
❑	❑	For shelves	____	____	____	____
❑	❑	For bookcases	____	____	____	____
❑	❑	Floral pieces	____	____	____	____
❑	❑	Candlesticks	____	____	____	____
❑	❑	Picture collections	____	____	____	____
❑	❑	____	____	____	____	____
❑	❑	____	____	____	____	____

A. Living Room (cont.)

Need	Have	Item	#	Size of Area	Color Scheme	Style/ Motif
Accessories:						
		Fireplace area —				
❑	❑	Andirons	___	___	___	___
❑	❑	Fireplace screen	___	___	___	___
❑	❑	Fireplace tools	___	___	___	___
❑	❑	Log holder	___	___	___	___
❑	❑	___	___	___	___	___
❑	❑	___	___	___	___	___
		Free standing —				
❑	❑	Plants	___	___	___	___
❑	❑	Baskets/pots	___	___	___	___
❑	❑	Magazine rack	___	___	___	___
❑	❑	___	___	___	___	___
❑	❑	___	___	___	___	___
❑	❑	___	___	___	___	___
❑	❑	___	___	___	___	___
		Linens —				
❑	❑	Table mats	___	___	___	___
❑	❑	Throw pillows	___	___	___	___
❑	❑	___	___	___	___	___
		Other —				
❑	❑	Wastebasket	___	___	___	___
❑	❑	Ashtrays	___	___	___	___
❑	❑	___	___	___	___	___
❑	❑	___	___	___	___	___
❑	❑	___	___	___	___	___
❑	❑	___	___	___	___	___
❑	❑	___	___	___	___	___
❑	❑	___	___	___	___	___
❑	❑	___	___	___	___	___

PLANNING GUIDES — DETAILED BY ROOM

B. Dining Room

Dominant Color(s): ________________

Need	Have	Item	#	Size	Color	Style
Furniture:						
❑	❑	Dining table	____	________	________	________
❑	❑	Dining chairs	____	________	________	________
❑	❑	Side chairs	____	________	________	________
❑	❑	Sideboard	____	________	________	________
❑	❑	Hutch	____	________	________	________
❑	❑	Serving cart	____	________	________	________
❑	❑	Counter stools	____	________	________	________
❑	❑	________	____	________	________	________
❑	❑	________	____	________	________	________
❑	❑	________	____	________	________	________
Lighting:						
❑	❑	Chandelier	____	________	________	________
❑	❑	Sconces	____	________	________	________
❑	❑	________	____	________	________	________
❑	❑	________	____	________	________	________
Flooring:						
❑	❑	Carpets				
❑	❑	Area rugs				
❑	❑	Tile/sheet goods				
❑	❑	________	____	________	________	________
❑	❑	________	____	________	________	________
Windows:						
❑	❑	Drapes/valances	____	________*	________	________
❑	❑	Curtains	____	________*	________	________
❑	❑	Blinds/shades	____	________*	________	________
❑	❑	________	____	________	________	________
❑	❑	________	____	________	________	________

* See pages 15 and 16 for precise sizes

B. Dining Room (cont.)

Need	Have	Item	#	Size	Color	Style
❑	❑	Drape/curtain rods	____	____________*	____________	____________
❑	❑	____________	____	____________	____________	____________
❑	❑	____________	____	____________	____________	____________
❑	❑	____________	____	____________	____________	____________

Need	Have	Item	#	Size of Area	Color Scheme	Style/ Motif
Accessories:						
		Wall hangings —				
❑	❑	Over sideboard	____	____________	____________	____________
❑	❑	Wall area "A"	____	____________	____________	____________
❑	❑	Wall area "B"	____	____________	____________	____________
❑	❑	Wall area "C"	____	____________	____________	____________
❑	❑	Wall area "D"	____	____________	____________	____________
❑	❑	Wall area "E"	____	____________	____________	____________
		Linens —				
❑	❑	Tablecloth/mats	____	____________	____________	____________
❑	❑	Napkins	____	____________	____________	____________
❑	❑	____________	____	____________	____________	____________
❑	❑	____________	____	____________	____________	____________
		Tabletop items —				
❑	❑	Table centerpiece	____	____________	____________	____________
❑	❑	Sideboard top	____	____________	____________	____________
❑	❑	Hutch top	____	____________	____________	____________
❑	❑	Candlesticks	____	____________	____________	____________
❑	❑	____________	____	____________	____________	____________
		Other —				
❑	❑	____________	____	____________	____________	____________
❑	❑	____________	____	____________	____________	____________
❑	❑	____________	____	____________	____________	____________

* See pages 15 and 16 for precise sizes

PLANNING GUIDES — DETAILED BY ROOM

C. Family Room

Dominant Color(s): ______________________

Need	Have	Item	#	Size	Color	Style
Furniture:						
❑	❑	Sofas	____	____________	____________	____________
❑	❑	Love seats	____	____________	____________	____________
❑	❑	Upholstered chairs	____	____________	____________	____________
❑	❑	Ottomans	____	____________	____________	____________
❑	❑	Side chairs	____	____________	____________	____________
❑	❑	Coffee tables	____	____________	____________	____________
❑	❑	End tables	____	____________	____________	____________
❑	❑	Sofa back tables	____	____________	____________	____________
❑	❑	Lamp tables	____	____________	____________	____________
❑	❑	TV cabinet/stand	____	____________	____________	____________
❑	❑	Bookcases	____	____________	____________	____________
❑	❑	Shelf units	____	____________	____________	____________
❑	❑	Display cabinets	____	____________	____________	____________
❑	❑	Storage cabinets	____	____________	____________	____________
❑	❑	Desk	____	____________	____________	____________
❑	❑	Desk chair	____	____________	____________	____________
❑	❑	Bench	____	____________	____________	____________
❑	❑	Game table/chairs	____	____________	____________	____________
❑	❑	Audio cabinet	____	____________	____________	____________
❑	❑	____________	____	____________	____________	____________
❑	❑	____________	____	____________	____________	____________
Lighting:						
❑	❑	Table lamps	____	____________	____________	____________
❑	❑	Floor lamps	____	____________	____________	____________
❑	❑	Wall lamps	____	____________	____________	____________
❑	❑	Ceiling lamps	____	____________	____________	____________
❑	❑	____________	____	____________	____________	____________
❑	❑	____________	____	____________	____________	____________

C. Family Room (cont.)

Need	Have	Item	#	Size	Color	Style
❑	❑	Picture lamps	____	____________	____________	________________
❑	❑	Desk lamp	____	____________	____________	________________
❑	❑	____________	____	____________	____________	________________
❑	❑	____________	____	____________	____________	________________
❑	❑	____________	____	____________	____________	________________
<u>Flooring:</u>						
❑	❑	Carpets	____	____________	____________	________________
❑	❑	Area rugs	____	____________	____________	________________
❑	❑	Tile/sheet goods	____	____________	____________	________________
❑	❑	____________	____	____________	____________	________________
❑	❑	____________	____	____________	____________	________________
<u>Windows:</u>						
❑	❑	Drapes/valances	____	____________*	____________	________________
❑	❑	Curtains	____	____________*	____________	________________
❑	❑	Blinds/shades	____	____________*	____________	________________
❑	❑	Drape/curtain rods	____	____________*	____________	________________
❑	❑	____________	____	____________	____________	________________
❑	❑	____________	____	____________	____________	________________
<u>Electronics:</u>						
❑	❑	Television set	____	____________	____________	________________
❑	❑	VCR	____	____________	____________	________________
❑	❑	Audio system	____	____________	____________	________________
❑	❑	Telephone	____	____________	____________	________________
❑	❑	____________	____	____________	____________	________________
<u>Other:</u>						
❑	❑	____________	____	____________	____________	________________
❑	❑	____________	____	____________	____________	________________
❑	❑	____________	____	____________	____________	________________
❑	❑	____________	____	____________	____________	________________
❑	❑	____________	____	____________	____________	________________

* See pages 15 and 16 for precise sizes

C. Family Room (cont.)

Need	Have	Item	#	Size of Area	Color Scheme	Style/ Motif
Accessories:						
		Wall hangings —				
❑	❑	Over mantle	____	____	____	____
❑	❑	Over couch	____	____	____	____
❑	❑	Above cabinet	____	____	____	____
❑	❑	Wall area "A"	____	____	____	____
❑	❑	Wall area "B"	____	____	____	____
❑	❑	Wall area "C"	____	____	____	____
❑	❑	Wall area "D"	____	____	____	____
❑	❑	Wall area "E"	____	____	____	____
❑	❑	Mirrors	____	____	____	____
❑	❑	Pictures	____	____	____	____
❑	❑	Clock	____	____	____	____
❑	❑	Plaques	____	____	____	____
❑	❑	____	____	____	____	____
❑	❑	____	____	____	____	____
❑	❑	____	____	____	____	____
		Tabletop items —				
❑	❑	Mantle top	____	____	____	____
❑	❑	Coffee table top	____	____	____	____
❑	❑	End table tops	____	____	____	____
❑	❑	Sofa table top	____	____	____	____
❑	❑	Cabinet tops	____	____	____	____
❑	❑	Desk accessories	____	____	____	____
❑	❑	For shelves	____	____	____	____
❑	❑	For bookcases	____	____	____	____
❑	❑	Floral pieces	____	____	____	____
❑	❑	Candlesticks	____	____	____	____
❑	❑	Picture collections	____	____	____	____
❑	❑	____	____	____	____	____

C. Family Room (cont.)

Need	Have	Item	#	Size of Area	Color Scheme	Style/ Motif
Accessories:						
		Fireplace area —				
❑	❑	Andirons				
❑	❑	Fireplace screen				
❑	❑	Fireplace tools				
❑	❑	Log holder				
❑	❑					
❑	❑					
		Free standing —				
❑	❑	Plants				
❑	❑	Baskets/pots				
❑	❑	Magazine rack				
❑	❑					
❑	❑					
❑	❑					
❑	❑					
		Linens —				
❑	❑	Table mats				
❑	❑	Throw pillows				
❑	❑					
❑	❑					
❑	❑					
		Other —				
❑	❑	Wastebasket				
❑	❑	Ashtrays				
❑	❑	Games				
❑	❑					
❑	❑					
❑	❑					
❑	❑					

PLANNING GUIDES — DETAILED BY ROOM

D. Study/Home Office

Dominant Color(s): ______________________

Need	Have	Item	#	Size	Color	Style
Furniture:						
❑	❑	Desk/chair	____	____________	____________	______________
❑	❑	Sofa	____	____________	____________	______________
❑	❑	Upholstered chairs	____	____________	____________	______________
❑	❑	Side chairs	____	____________	____________	______________
❑	❑	Coffee table	____	____________	____________	______________
❑	❑	End tables	____	____________	____________	______________
❑	❑	Lamp tables	____	____________	____________	______________
❑	❑	Bookcases	____	____________	____________	______________
❑	❑	File cabinets	____	____________	____________	______________
❑	❑	Storage cabinets	____	____________	____________	______________
❑	❑	______________	____	____________	____________	______________
❑	❑	______________	____	____________	____________	______________
❑	❑	______________	____	____________	____________	______________
Lighting:						
❑	❑	Table lamps	____	____________	____________	______________
❑	❑	Desk lamp	____	____________	____________	______________
❑	❑	Floor lamps	____	____________	____________	______________
❑	❑	Picture lamps	____	____________	____________	______________
Flooring:						
❑	❑	Carpet/area rugs	____	____________	____________	______________
Windows:						
❑	❑	Drapes/valances	____	____________*	____________	______________
❑	❑	Curtains	____	____________*	____________	______________
❑	❑	Blinds/shades	____	____________*	____________	______________
❑	❑	Drapes/curtain rods	____	____________*	____________	______________
❑	❑	______________	____	____________	____________	______________
❑	❑	______________	____	____________	____________	______________

* See pages 15 and 16 for precise sizes

D. Study/Home Office (cont.)

Need	Have	Item	#	Size	Color	Style
Electronics:						
❑	❑	Telephone	____	____	____	____
❑	❑	Answering machine	____	____	____	____
❑	❑	Fax	____	____	____	____
❑	❑	Computer	____	____	____	____
❑	❑	Audio system	____	____	____	____

Need	Have	Item	#	Size of Area	Color Scheme	Style/ Motif
Accessories:						
		Wall hangings —				
❑	❑	Wall area "A"	____	____	____	____
❑	❑	Wall area "B"	____	____	____	____
❑	❑	Wall area "C"	____	____	____	____
❑	❑	Wall area "D"	____	____	____	____
		Tabletop items —				
❑	❑	Desk accessories	____	____	____	____
❑	❑	Coffee table top	____	____	____	____
❑	❑	End table tops	____	____	____	____
❑	❑	For bookcases	____	____	____	____
❑	❑	Cabinet tops	____	____	____	____
❑	❑	____	____	____	____	____
❑	❑	____	____	____	____	____
		Other —				
❑	❑	Wastebasket	____	____	____	____
❑	❑	Ashtrays	____	____	____	____
❑	❑	____	____	____	____	____
❑	❑	____	____	____	____	____
❑	❑	____	____	____	____	____
❑	❑	____	____	____	____	____
❑	❑	____	____	____	____	____

PLANNING GUIDES — DETAILED BY ROOM

E. Foyer

Dominant Color(s): ____________________

Need	Have	Item	#	Size	Color	Style
Furniture:						
❑	❑	Cabinet/table	____	____________	____________	____________
❑	❑	Bench	____	____________	____________	____________
Lighting:						
❑	❑	Ceiling/wall lamps	____	____________	____________	____________
❑	❑	Cabinet top lamp	____	____________	____________	____________
Flooring:						
❑	❑	Area rug/floor mat	____	____________	____________	____________
Windows:						
❑	❑	Curtains/rods	____	____________ *	____________	____________
❑	❑	Blinds/shades	____	____________ *	____________	____________
Accessories:						
❑	❑	Wall hangings	____	____________	____________	____________
❑	❑	Cabinet/tabletop	____	____________	____________	____________
❑	❑	____________	____	____________	____________	____________

F. Hallway

Dominant Color(s): ____________________

Need	Have	Item	#	Size	Color	Style
Lighting:						
❑	❑	Ceiling/wall lamps	____	____________	____________	____________
Flooring:						
❑	❑	Carpet/runner	____	____________	____________	____________
Windows:						
❑	❑	Curtains/rods	____	____________ *	____________	____________
❑	❑	Blinds/shades	____	____________ *	____________	____________
Accessories:						
❑	❑	Wall hangings	____	____________	____________	____________
❑	❑	____________	____	____________	____________	____________

* See pages 15 and 16 for precise sizes

PLANNING GUIDES — DETAILED BY ROOM

G. Kitchen

Dominant Color(s): ____________________

Need	Have	Item	#	Size	Color	Style
Appliances:						
❏	❏	Refrigerator	____	____________	____________	____________
❏	❏	Cook top/range	____	____________	____________	____________
❏	❏	Oven	____	____________	____________	____________
❏	❏	Compactor	____	____________	____________	____________
❏	❏	Microwave	____	____________	____________	____________
❏	❏	Toaster oven	____	____________	____________	____________
❏	❏	Toaster	____	____________	____________	____________
❏	❏	Food processor	____	____________	____________	____________
❏	❏	Blender	____	____________	____________	____________
❏	❏	Coffeemaker	____	____________	____________	____________
❏	❏	____________	____	____________	____________	____________
Electronics:						
❏	❏	Telephone	____	____________	____________	____________
❏	❏	Answering machine	____	____________	____________	____________
❏	❏	Clock	____	____________	____________	____________
❏	❏	____________	____	____________	____________	____________
Furniture:						
❏	❏	Table	____	____________	____________	____________
❏	❏	Chairs	____	____________	____________	____________
❏	❏	Storage cabinets	____	____________	____________	____________
❏	❏	Counter stools	____	____________	____________	____________
Lighting:						
❏	❏	Ceiling/wall lamps	____	____________	____________	____________
❏	❏	Task area lights	____	____________	____________	____________
❏	❏	Table lamp	____	____________	____________	____________
❏	❏	____________	____	____________	____________	____________
❏	❏	____________	____	____________	____________	____________
❏	❏	____________	____	____________	____________	____________

G. Kitchen (cont.)

Need	Have	Item	#	Size	Color	Style
Windows:						
❑	❑	Curtains/rods	____	____________ *	____________	____________
❑	❑	Blinds/shades	____	____________ *	____________	____________
❑	❑	____________	____	____________	____________	____________

Need	Have	Item	#	Size of Area	Color Scheme	Style/ Motif
Accessories:						
		Wall hangings —				
❑	❑	Wall area "A"	____	____________	____________	____________
❑	❑	Wall area "B"	____	____________	____________	____________
❑	❑	Wall area "C"	____	____________	____________	____________
❑	❑	Wall area "D"	____	____________	____________	____________
❑	❑	____________	____	____________	____________	____________
❑	❑	____________	____	____________	____________	____________
		Other —				
❑	❑	Tabletop items	____	____________	____________	____________
❑	❑	Candlesticks	____	____________	____________	____________
❑	❑	Towel racks	____	____________	____________	____________
❑	❑	Soap dishes	____	____________	____________	____________
❑	❑	Bulletin board	____	____________	____________	____________
❑	❑	Paper towel holder	____	____________	____________	____________
❑	❑	____________	____	____________	____________	____________
❑	❑	____________	____	____________	____________	____________
❑	❑	____________	____	____________	____________	____________
❑	❑	____________	____	____________	____________	____________
❑	❑	____________	____	____________	____________	____________
❑	❑	____________	____	____________	____________	____________
❑	❑	____________	____	____________	____________	____________
❑	❑	____________	____	____________	____________	____________
❑	❑	____________	____	____________	____________	____________

* See pages 15 and 16 for precise sizes

G. Kitchen (cont.) - Housewares

Need	Have	Item	#/Style
Servingware:			
❑	❑	China (good)	________
❑	❑	Glasses (good)	________
❑	❑	Salad bowl (good)	________
❑	❑	Breadbasket (good)	________
❑	❑	Ice bucket	________
❑	❑	Wine glasses	________
❑	❑	Wine cooler	________
❑	❑	Serving trays	________
❑	❑	Coasters	________
❑	❑	Salt/pepper shakers	________
❑	❑	China (everyday)	________
❑	❑	Glasses (everyday)	________
❑	❑	Vegetable bowls	________
❑	❑	Platters	________
❑	❑	Salad bowl/servers	________
❑	❑	Bread baskets	________
❑	❑	Pitchers	________
❑	❑	Butter dishes	________
❑	❑	Napkin holder	________
❑	❑	Cheese boards	________
❑	❑	Snack bowls	________
❑	❑	________	________
❑	❑	________	________
❑	❑	________	________
❑	❑	________	________
❑	❑	________	________
❑	❑	________	________
❑	❑	________	________
❑	❑	________	________

Need	Have	Item	#/Style
Flatware:			
❑	❑	Place settings*	________
❑	❑	Hostess set*	________
❑	❑	Place sets**	________
❑	❑	Hostess set**	________
❑	❑	________	________
❑	❑	________	________
		*good **everyday	
Cookware:			
❑	❑	Skillets/lids	________
❑	❑	Pots/lids	________
❑	❑	Stock pot/lid	________
❑	❑	Steamer rack	________
❑	❑	Tea kettle	________
❑	❑	Roasting pans	________
❑	❑	Griddle	________
❑	❑	Baking dishes	________
❑	❑	Baking pans	________
❑	❑	Cookie sheets	________
❑	❑	Mixing bowls	________
❑	❑	Colanders	________
❑	❑	Measuring cups	________
❑	❑	Strainers	________
❑	❑	Funnels	________
❑	❑	Ricer/masher	________
❑	❑	Juicer	________
❑	❑	Cutting boards	________
❑	❑	________	________
❑	❑	________	________
❑	❑	________	________

G. Kitchen (cont.) - Housewares

Utensils:

Need	Have	Item	#/Style
❑	❑	Carving set	________
❑	❑	Steak knives	________
❑	❑	Utensil set/rack	________
❑	❑	Spatulas	________
❑	❑	Tongs	________
❑	❑	Pasta server	________
❑	❑	Spreader	________
❑	❑	Whisks/beaters	________
❑	❑	Grill set	________
❑	❑	Measuring spoons	________
❑	❑	Measuring cups	________
❑	❑	Ladles	________
❑	❑	Grater	________
❑	❑	Vegetable scraper	________
❑	❑	Vegetable brush	________
❑	❑	Corkscrew	________
❑	❑	Bottle opener	________
❑	❑	Can opener	________
❑	❑	Mallet	________
❑	❑	Cheese slicers	________
❑	❑	Ice cream scoop	________
❑	❑	Skewers	________
❑	❑	________	________
❑	❑	________	________
❑	❑	________	________
❑	❑	________	________
❑	❑	________	________
❑	❑	________	________
❑	❑	________	________

Containers:

Need	Have	Item	#/Style
❑	❑	Plastic containers	________
❑	❑	Juice pitchers	________
❑	❑	Canister set	________
❑	❑	Ice cube trays/bin	________
❑	❑	________	________
❑	❑	________	________
❑	❑	________	________

Linens:

Need	Have	Item	#/Style
❑	❑	Tablecloths	________
❑	❑	Napkins	________
❑	❑	Placemats	________
❑	❑	Patio table set	________
❑	❑	Dish towels	________
❑	❑	Hand towels	________
❑	❑	Aprons	________
❑	❑	Pot holders	________
❑	❑	Trivets	________
❑	❑	Hot pads	________
❑	❑	________	________
❑	❑	________	________

Other:

Need	Have	Item	#/Style
❑	❑	Dish drainer	________
❑	❑	Timer	________
❑	❑	Candle snuffer	________
❑	❑	________	________
❑	❑	________	________
❑	❑	________	________
❑	❑	________	________
❑	❑	________	________

PLANNING GUIDES — DETAILED BY ROOM

H. Pantry/Utility Closet

Dominant Color(s): ________________

Need	Have	Item	#	Size	Color	Style
Appliances:						
❑	❑	Vacuum	____	________	________	________
❑	❑	________	____	________	________	________
Furniture:						
❑	❑	Storage cabinets	____	________	________	________
❑	❑	Shelving	____	________	________	________
❑	❑	________	____	________	________	________
❑	❑	________	____	________	________	________
❑	❑	________	____	________	________	________
Windows:						
❑	❑	Curtains/rods	____	________*	________	________
❑	❑	Blinds/shades	____	________*	________	________
❑	❑	________	____	________	________	________
Other:						
❑	❑	Wall hooks	____	________	________	________
❑	❑	Brooms	____	________	________	________
❑	❑	Mops	____	________	________	________
❑	❑	Dustpan/brushes	____	________	________	________
❑	❑	Bucket/brushes	____	________	________	________
❑	❑	Trash bins	____	________	________	________
❑	❑	Recyclable bins	____	________	________	________
❑	❑	Stepladder	____	________	________	________
❑	❑	Fire extinguisher	____	________	________	________
❑	❑	________	____	________	________	________
❑	❑	________	____	________	________	________
❑	❑	________	____	________	________	________
❑	❑	________	____	________	________	________

* See pages 15 and 16 for precise sizes

PLANNING GUIDES — DETAILED BY ROOM

I. Master Bedroom

Dominant Color(s): ______________________

Need	Have	Item	#	Size	Color	Style
Furniture:						
❑	❑	Bed/headboard	____	____________	____________	____________
❑	❑	Bureau (his)	____	____________	____________	____________
❑	❑	Bureau (hers)	____	____________	____________	____________
❑	❑	Bedside tables	____	____________	____________	____________
❑	❑	Side chairs/bench	____	____________	____________	____________
❑	❑	Blanket chest	____	____________	____________	____________
❑	❑	TV stand	____	____________	____________	____________
❑	❑	____________	____	____________	____________	____________
❑	❑	____________	____	____________	____________	____________
❑	❑	____________	____	____________	____________	____________
❑	❑	____________	____	____________	____________	____________
Lighting:						
❑	❑	Bedside lamps	____	____________	____________	____________
❑	❑	Bureau lamps	____	____________	____________	____________
❑	❑	Floor lamps	____	____________	____________	____________
❑	❑	Ceiling/wall lamps	____	____________	____________	____________
❑	❑	____________	____	____________	____________	____________
Flooring:						
❑	❑	Carpets/rugs	____	____________	____________	____________
❑	❑	____________	____	____________	____________	____________
Windows:						
❑	❑	Drapes/valances	____	____________*	____________	____________
❑	❑	Curtains	____	____________*	____________	____________
❑	❑	Blinds/shades	____	____________*	____________	____________
❑	❑	Drape/curtain rods	____	____________*	____________	____________
❑	❑	____________	____	____________	____________	____________
❑	❑	____________	____	____________	____________	____________

* See pages 15 and 16 for precise sizes

I. Master Bedroom (cont.)

Need	Have	Item	#	Size	Color	Style
Electronics:						
❑	❑	Clock radio	____	________	________	________
❑	❑	Television set	____	________	________	________
❑	❑	Telephone	____	________	________	________
❑	❑	________	____	________	________	________

Need	Have	Item	#	Size of Area	Color Scheme	Style/ Motif
Accessories:						
		Wall hangings —				
❑	❑	Above bed	____	________	________	________
❑	❑	Wall area "A"	____	________	________	________
❑	❑	Wall area "B"	____	________	________	________
❑	❑	Wall area "C"	____	________	________	________
❑	❑	Wall area "D"	____	________	________	________
❑	❑	Mirrors	____	________	________	________
		Bedding/linens —				
❑	❑	Mattress/springs	____	________	________	________
❑	❑	Pillows	____	________	________	________
❑	❑	Sheets/pillowcases	____	________	________	________
❑	❑	Blankets/quilts	____	________	________	________
❑	❑	Mattress covers	____	________	________	________
❑	❑	Bedspread/shams	____	________	________	________
❑	❑	Dresser mats	____	________	________	________
		Tabletop items —				
❑	❑	Bureau tops	____	________	________	________
❑	❑	Bedside table tops	____	________	________	________
❑	❑	________	____	________	________	________
❑	❑	________	____	________	________	________
❑	❑	________	____	________	________	________
❑	❑	________	____	________	________	________

I. Master Bedroom (cont.)

Need	Have	Item	#	Size	Color	Style
		Other accessories —				
❑	❑	Bedspread rack	____	____	____	____
❑	❑	Wastebasket	____	____	____	____
❑	❑	Flashlight	____	____	____	____
❑	❑	____	____	____	____	____
❑	❑	____	____	____	____	____
❑	❑	____	____	____	____	____
Closet:						
❑	❑	Shelving	____	____	____	____
❑	❑	Shoe rack	____	____	____	____
❑	❑	Tie rack	____	____	____	____
❑	❑	Wall hooks	____	____	____	____
❑	❑	Hangers	____	____	____	____
❑	❑	Hamper	____	____	____	____
❑	❑	____	____	____	____	____
❑	❑	____	____	____	____	____
❑	❑	____	____	____	____	____
❑	❑	____	____	____	____	____
❑	❑	____	____	____	____	____
Other:						
❑	❑	____	____	____	____	____
❑	❑	____	____	____	____	____
❑	❑	____	____	____	____	____
❑	❑	____	____	____	____	____
❑	❑	____	____	____	____	____
❑	❑	____	____	____	____	____
❑	❑	____	____	____	____	____
❑	❑	____	____	____	____	____

PLANNING GUIDES — DETAILED BY ROOM

J. Bedroom #2

Dominant Color(s): ______________________

Need	Have	Item	#	Size	Color	Style
Furniture:						
❑	❑	Bed/headboard	____	____________	____________	________________
❑	❑	Bureau (his)	____	____________	____________	________________
❑	❑	Bureau (hers)	____	____________	____________	________________
❑	❑	Bedside tables	____	____________	____________	________________
❑	❑	Side chairs/bench	____	____________	____________	________________
❑	❑	Blanket chest	____	____________	____________	________________
❑	❑	TV stand	____	____________	____________	________________
❑	❑	____________	____	____________	____________	________________
❑	❑	____________	____	____________	____________	________________
❑	❑	____________	____	____________	____________	________________
❑	❑	____________	____	____________	____________	________________
Lighting:						
❑	❑	Bedside lamps	____	____________	____________	________________
❑	❑	Bureau lamps	____	____________	____________	________________
❑	❑	Floor lamps	____	____________	____________	________________
❑	❑	Ceiling/wall lamps	____	____________	____________	________________
❑	❑	____________	____	____________	____________	________________
Flooring:						
❑	❑	Carpets/rugs	____	____________	____________	________________
❑	❑	____________	____	____________	____________	________________
Windows:						
❑	❑	Drapes/valances	____	____________*	____________	________________
❑	❑	Curtains	____	____________*	____________	________________
❑	❑	Blinds/shades	____	____________*	____________	________________
❑	❑	Drape/curtain rods	____	____________*	____________	________________
❑	❑	____________	____	____________	____________	________________
❑	❑	____________	____	____________	____________	________________

* See pages 15 and 16 for precise sizes

J. Bedroom #2 (cont.)

Need	Have	Item	#	Size	Color	Style
Electronics:						
❑	❑	Clock radio	____	________	________	________
❑	❑	Television set	____	________	________	________
❑	❑	Telephone	____	________	________	________
❑	❑	________	____	________	________	________

Need	Have	Item	#	Size of Area	Color Scheme	Style/ Motif
Accessories:						
		Wall hangings —				
❑	❑	Above bed	____	________	________	________
❑	❑	Wall area "A"	____	________	________	________
❑	❑	Wall area "B"	____	________	________	________
❑	❑	Wall area "C"	____	________	________	________
❑	❑	Wall area "D"	____	________	________	________
❑	❑	Mirrors	____	________	________	________
		Bedding/linens —				
❑	❑	Mattress/springs	____	________	________	________
❑	❑	Pillows	____	________	________	________
❑	❑	Sheets/pillowcases	____	________	________	________
❑	❑	Blankets/quilts	____	________	________	________
❑	❑	Mattress covers	____	________	________	________
❑	❑	Bedspread/shams	____	________	________	________
❑	❑	Dresser mats	____	________	________	________
❑	❑	________	____	________	________	________
		Tabletop items —				
❑	❑	Bureau tops	____	________	________	________
❑	❑	Bedside table tops	____	________	________	________
❑	❑	________	____	________	________	________
❑	❑	________	____	________	________	________
❑	❑	________	____	________	________	________

J. Bedroom #2 (cont.)

Need	Have	Item	#	Size	Color	Style/
		Other accessories —				
❑	❑	Bedspread rack	____	____	____	____
❑	❑	Wastebasket	____	____	____	____
❑	❑	Flashlight	____	____	____	____
❑	❑	____	____	____	____	____
❑	❑	____	____	____	____	____
❑	❑	____	____	____	____	____
Closet:						
❑	❑	Shelving	____	____	____	____
❑	❑	Shoe rack	____	____	____	____
❑	❑	Tie rack	____	____	____	____
❑	❑	Wall hooks	____	____	____	____
❑	❑	Hangers	____	____	____	____
❑	❑	Hamper	____	____	____	____
❑	❑	____	____	____	____	____
❑	❑	____	____	____	____	____
❑	❑	____	____	____	____	____
❑	❑	____	____	____	____	____
❑	❑	____	____	____	____	____
Other:						
❑	❑	____	____	____	____	____
❑	❑	____	____	____	____	____
❑	❑	____	____	____	____	____
❑	❑	____	____	____	____	____
❑	❑	____	____	____	____	____
❑	❑	____	____	____	____	____
❑	❑	____	____	____	____	____
❑	❑	____	____	____	____	____
❑	❑	____	____	____	____	____
❑	❑	____	____	____	____	____
❑	❑	____	____	____	____	____

PLANNING GUIDES — DETAILED BY ROOM

K. Bedroom #3

Dominant Color(s): ______________________

Need	Have	Item	#	Size	Color	Style
Furniture:						
❑	❑	Bed/headboard				
❑	❑	Bureau (his)				
❑	❑	Bureau (hers)				
❑	❑	Bedside tables				
❑	❑	Side chairs/bench				
❑	❑	Blanket chest				
❑	❑	TV stand				
❑	❑					
❑	❑					
❑	❑					
❑	❑					
Lighting:						
❑	❑	Bedside lamps				
❑	❑	Bureau lamps				
❑	❑	Floor lamps				
❑	❑	Ceiling/wall lamps				
❑	❑					
Flooring:						
❑	❑	Carpets/rugs				
❑	❑					
Windows:						
❑	❑	Drapes/valances		*		
❑	❑	Curtains		*		
❑	❑	Blinds/shades		*		
❑	❑	Drape/curtain rods		*		
❑	❑					
❑	❑					

* See pages 15 and 16 for precise sizes

K. Bedroom #3 (cont.)

Need	Have	Item	#	Size	Color	Style
Electronics:						
❑	❑	Clock radio	____	________	________	________
❑	❑	Television set	____	________	________	________
❑	❑	Telephone	____	________	________	________
❑	❑	________	____	________	________	________

Need	Have	Item	#	Size of Area	Color Scheme	Style/ Motif
Accessories:						
		Wall hangings —				
❑	❑	Above bed	____	________	________	________
❑	❑	Wall area "A"	____	________	________	________
❑	❑	Wall area "B"	____	________	________	________
❑	❑	Wall area "C"	____	________	________	________
❑	❑	Wall area "D"	____	________	________	________
❑	❑	Mirrors	____	________	________	________
		Bedding/linens —				
❑	❑	Mattress/springs	____	________	________	________
❑	❑	Pillows	____	________	________	________
❑	❑	Sheets/pillowcases	____	________	________	________
❑	❑	Blankets/quilts	____	________	________	________
❑	❑	Mattress covers	____	________	________	________
❑	❑	Bedspread/shams	____	________	________	________
❑	❑	Dresser mats	____	________	________	________
❑	❑	________	____	________	________	________
		Tabletop items —				
❑	❑	Bureau tops	____	________	________	________
❑	❑	Bedside table tops	____	________	________	________
❑	❑	________	____	________	________	________
❑	❑	________	____	________	________	________
❑	❑	________	____	________	________	________

K. Bedroom #3 (cont.)

Need	Have	Item	#	Size	Color	Style/
		Other accessories —				
❑	❑	Bedspread rack				
❑	❑	Wastebasket				
❑	❑	Flashlight				
❑	❑					
❑	❑					
❑	❑					
Closet:						
❑	❑	Shelving				
❑	❑	Shoe rack				
❑	❑	Tie rack				
❑	❑	Wall hooks				
❑	❑	Hangers				
❑	❑	Hamper				
❑	❑					
❑	❑					
❑	❑					
❑	❑					
❑	❑					
Other:						
❑	❑					
❑	❑					
❑	❑					
❑	❑					
❑	❑					
❑	❑					
❑	❑					
❑	❑					
❑	❑					
❑	❑					
❑	❑					

PLANNING GUIDES — DETAILED BY ROOM

L. Bedroom #4

Dominant Color(s): ______________________

Need	Have	Item	#	Size	Color	Style
Furniture:						
❑	❑	Bed/headboard	____	________	________	________
❑	❑	Bureau (his)	____	________	________	________
❑	❑	Bureau (hers)	____	________	________	________
❑	❑	Bedside tables	____	________	________	________
❑	❑	Side chairs/bench	____	________	________	________
❑	❑	Blanket chest	____	________	________	________
❑	❑	TV stand	____	________	________	________
❑	❑	________	____	________	________	________
❑	❑	________	____	________	________	________
❑	❑	________	____	________	________	________
❑	❑	________	____	________	________	________
Lighting:						
❑	❑	Bedside lamps	____	________	________	________
❑	❑	Bureau lamps	____	________	________	________
❑	❑	Floor lamps	____	________	________	________
❑	❑	Ceiling/wall lamps	____	________	________	________
❑	❑	________	____	________	________	________
Flooring:						
❑	❑	Carpets/rugs	____	________	________	________
❑	❑	________	____	________	________	________
Windows:						
❑	❑	Drapes/valances	____	________*	________	________
❑	❑	Curtains	____	________*	________	________
❑	❑	Blinds/shades	____	________*	________	________
❑	❑	Drape/curtain rods	____	________*	________	________
❑	❑	________	____	________	________	________
❑	❑	________	____	________	________	________

* See pages 15 and 16 for precise sizes

L. Bedroom #4 (cont.)

Need	Have	Item	#	Size	Color	Style
Electronics:						
❑	❑	Clock radio	____	____________	____________	________________
❑	❑	Television set	____	____________	____________	________________
❑	❑	Telephone	____	____________	____________	________________
❑	❑	____________	____	____________	____________	________________

Need	Have	Item	#	Size of Area	Color Scheme	Style/ Motif
Accessories:						
		Wall hangings —				
❑	❑	Above bed	____	____________	____________	________________
❑	❑	Wall area "A"	____	____________	____________	________________
❑	❑	Wall area "B"	____	____________	____________	________________
❑	❑	Wall area "C"	____	____________	____________	________________
❑	❑	Wall area "D"	____	____________	____________	________________
❑	❑	Mirrors	____	____________	____________	________________
		Bedding/linens —				
❑	❑	Mattress/springs	____	____________	____________	________________
❑	❑	Pillows	____	____________	____________	________________
❑	❑	Sheets/pillowcases	____	____________	____________	________________
❑	❑	Blankets/quilts	____	____________	____________	________________
❑	❑	Mattress covers	____	____________	____________	________________
❑	❑	Bedspread/shams	____	____________	____________	________________
❑	❑	Dresser mats	____	____________	____________	________________
❑	❑	____________	____	____________	____________	________________
		Tabletop items —				
❑	❑	Bureau tops	____	____________	____________	________________
❑	❑	Bedside table tops	____	____________	____________	________________
❑	❑	____________	____	____________	____________	________________
❑	❑	____________	____	____________	____________	________________
❑	❑	____________	____	____________	____________	________________

L. Bedroom #4 (cont.)

Need	Have	Item	#	Size	Color	Style/
		Other accessories —				
❑	❑	Bedspread rack	____	____	____	____
❑	❑	Wastebasket	____	____	____	____
❑	❑	Flashlight	____	____	____	____
❑	❑	____	____	____	____	____
❑	❑	____	____	____	____	____
❑	❑	____	____	____	____	____
Closet:						
❑	❑	Shelving	____	____	____	____
❑	❑	Shoe rack	____	____	____	____
❑	❑	Tie rack	____	____	____	____
❑	❑	Wall hooks	____	____	____	____
❑	❑	Hangers	____	____	____	____
❑	❑	Hamper	____	____	____	____
❑	❑	____	____	____	____	____
❑	❑	____	____	____	____	____
❑	❑	____	____	____	____	____
❑	❑	____	____	____	____	____
❑	❑	____	____	____	____	____
Other:						
❑	❑	____	____	____	____	____
❑	❑	____	____	____	____	____
❑	❑	____	____	____	____	____
❑	❑	____	____	____	____	____
❑	❑	____	____	____	____	____
❑	❑	____	____	____	____	____
❑	❑	____	____	____	____	____
❑	❑	____	____	____	____	____
❑	❑	____	____	____	____	____
❑	❑	____	____	____	____	____
❑	❑	____	____	____	____	____

PLANNING GUIDES — DETAILED BY ROOM

M. Master Bathroom

Dominant Color(s): ______________________

Need	Have	Item	#	Size	Color	Style
Accessories:						
❑	❑	Medicine cabinet	____	____	____	____
❑	❑	Towel racks	____	____	____	____
❑	❑	Toilet tissue holder	____	____	____	____
❑	❑	Door hooks	____	____	____	____
❑	❑	Soap dishes	____	____	____	____
❑	❑	Toothbrush holder	____	____	____	____
❑	❑	Mirrors	____	____	____	____
❑	❑	Wall hangings	____	____	____	____
❑	❑	Shower curtain/rings	____	____	____	____
❑	❑	Wastebasket	____	____	____	____
❑	❑	Scale	____	____	____	____
❑	❑	Hamper	____	____	____	____
❑	❑	Toilet brush/plunger	____	____	____	____
❑	❑	____	____	____	____	____
Lighting:						
❑	❑	Wall lamps	____	____	____	____
Windows:						
❑	❑	Curtains/rods	____	____ *	____	____
❑	❑	Blinds/shades	____	____ *	____	____
Linens:						
❑	❑	Towels/washcloths	____	____	____	____
❑	❑	Bath mat	____	____	____	____
Other:						
❑	❑	____	____	____	____	____
❑	❑	____	____	____	____	____
❑	❑	____	____	____	____	____
❑	❑	____	____	____	____	____

* See pages 15 and 16 for precise sizes

PLANNING GUIDES — DETAILED BY ROOM

N. Bathroom #2

Dominant Color(s): ____________________

Need	Have	Item	#	Size	Color	Style
Accessories:						
❑	❑	Medicine cabinet	____	________	________	________
❑	❑	Towel racks	____	________	________	________
❑	❑	Toilet tissue holder	____	________	________	________
❑	❑	Door hooks	____	________	________	________
❑	❑	Soap dishes	____	________	________	________
❑	❑	Toothbrush holder	____	________	________	________
❑	❑	Mirrors	____	________	________	________
❑	❑	Wall hangings	____	________	________	________
❑	❑	Shower curtain/rings	____	________	________	________
❑	❑	Wastebasket	____	________	________	________
❑	❑	Scale	____	________	________	________
❑	❑	Hamper	____	________	________	________
❑	❑	Toilet brush/plunger	____	________	________	________
❑	❑	________	____	________	________	________
Lighting:						
❑	❑	Wall lamps	____	________	________	________
Windows:						
❑	❑	Curtains/rods	____	________*	________	________
❑	❑	Blinds/shades	____	________*	________	________
Linens:						
❑	❑	Towels/washcloths	____	________	________	________
❑	❑	Bath mat	____	________	________	________
Other:						
❑	❑	________	____	________	________	________
❑	❑	________	____	________	________	________
❑	❑	________	____	________	________	________

* See pages 15 and 16 for precise sizes

PLANNING GUIDES — DETAILED BY ROOM

O. Bathroom #3

Dominant Color(s): ______

Need	Have	Item	#	Size	Color	Style
Accessories:						
❑	❑	Medicine cabinet	____	____	____	____
❑	❑	Towel racks	____	____	____	____
❑	❑	Toilet tissue holder	____	____	____	____
❑	❑	Door hooks	____	____	____	____
❑	❑	Soap dishes	____	____	____	____
❑	❑	Toothbrush holder	____	____	____	____
❑	❑	Mirrors	____	____	____	____
❑	❑	Wall hangings	____	____	____	____
❑	❑	Shower curtain/rings	____	____	____	____
❑	❑	Wastebasket	____	____	____	____
❑	❑	Scale	____	____	____	____
❑	❑	Hamper	____	____	____	____
❑	❑	Toilet brush/plunger	____	____	____	____
❑	❑	____	____	____	____	____
Lighting:						
❑	❑	Wall lamps	____	____	____	____
Windows:						
❑	❑	Curtains/rods	____	____ *	____	____
❑	❑	Blinds/shades	____	____ *	____	____
Linens:						
❑	❑	Towels/washcloths	____	____	____	____
❑	❑	Bath mat	____	____	____	____
Other:						
❑	❑	____	____	____	____	____
❑	❑	____	____	____	____	____
❑	❑	____	____	____	____	____
❑	❑	____	____	____	____	____

* See pages 15 and 16 for precise sizes

PLANNING GUIDES — DETAILED BY ROOM

P. Bathroom #4

Dominant Color(s): ______________________

Need	Have	Item	#	Size	Color	Style
Accessories:						
❑	❑	Medicine cabinet	____	________	________	________
❑	❑	Towel racks	____	________	________	________
❑	❑	Toilet tissue holder	____	________	________	________
❑	❑	Door hooks	____	________	________	________
❑	❑	Soap dishes	____	________	________	________
❑	❑	Toothbrush holder	____	________	________	________
❑	❑	Mirrors	____	________	________	________
❑	❑	Wall hangings	____	________	________	________
❑	❑	Shower curtain/rings	____	________	________	________
❑	❑	Wastebasket	____	________	________	________
❑	❑	Scale	____	________	________	________
❑	❑	Hamper	____	________	________	________
❑	❑	Toilet brush/plunger	____	________	________	________
❑	❑	________	____	________	________	________
Lighting:						
❑	❑	Wall lamps	____	________	________	________
Windows:						
❑	❑	Curtains/rods	____	________*	________	________
❑	❑	Blinds/shades	____	________*	________	________
Linens:						
❑	❑	Towels/washcloths	____	________	________	________
❑	❑	Bath mat	____	________	________	________
Other:						
❑	❑	________	____	________	________	________
❑	❑	________	____	________	________	________
❑	❑	________	____	________	________	________
❑	❑	________	____	________	________	________

* See pages 15 and 16 for precise sizes

PLANNING GUIDES — DETAILED BY ROOM

Q. Upstairs Hallway

Dominant Color(s): ______________________

Need	Have	Item	#	Size	Color	Style
Furniture:						
❑	❑	Cabinet	____	____________	____________	______________
❑	❑	Side chairs	____	____________	____________	______________
❑	❑	____________	____	____________	____________	______________
❑	❑	____________	____	____________	____________	______________
Lighting:						
❑	❑	Ceiling/wall lamps	____	____________	____________	______________
❑	❑	Cabinet top lamp	____	____________	____________	______________
❑	❑	____________	____	____________	____________	______________
❑	❑	____________	____	____________	____________	______________
Flooring:						
❑	❑	Carpet/runner	____	____________	____________	______________
❑	❑	____________	____	____________	____________	______________
❑	❑	____________	____	____________	____________	______________
Windows:						
❑	❑	Curtains/rods	____	____________*	____________	______________
❑	❑	Blinds/shades	____	____________*	____________	______________
❑	❑	____________	____	____________	____________	______________
Accessories:						
❑	❑	Wall hangings	____	____________	____________	______________
❑	❑	Cabinet top	____	____________	____________	______________
❑	❑	____________	____	____________	____________	______________
❑	❑	____________	____	____________	____________	______________
Other:						
❑	❑	____________	____	____________	____________	______________
❑	❑	____________	____	____________	____________	______________
❑	❑	____________	____	____________	____________	______________
❑	❑	____________	____	____________	____________	______________

* See pages 15 and 16 for precise sizes

PLANNING GUIDES — DETAILED BY ROOM

R. Laundry Room

Dominant Color(s): ______________________

Need	Have	Item	#	Size	Color	Style
Appliances:						
❏	❏	Washer	____	__________	__________	__________
❏	❏	Dryer	____	__________	__________	__________
❏	❏	Iron	____	__________	__________	__________
❏	❏	__________	____	__________	__________	__________
Furniture:						
❏	❏	Storage cabinets	____	__________	__________	__________
❏	❏	Shelving	____	__________	__________	__________
❏	❏	__________	____	__________	__________	__________
❏	❏	__________	____	__________	__________	__________
Flooring:						
❏	❏	Area rug	____	__________	__________	__________
❏	❏	Tile/sheet goods	____	__________	__________	__________
❏	❏	__________	____	__________	__________	__________
Lighting:						
❏	❏	Ceiling/wall lamps	____	__________	__________	__________
❏	❏	__________	____	__________	__________	__________
Windows:						
❏	❏	Curtains/rods	____	__________*	__________	__________
❏	❏	Blinds/shades	____	__________*	__________	__________
Accessories:						
❏	❏	Ironing board	____	__________	__________	__________
❏	❏	Hamper	____	__________	__________	__________
❏	❏	Clothes drying rack	____	__________	__________	__________
❏	❏	Clothespins/bag	____	__________	__________	__________
❏	❏	Wall hangings	____	__________	__________	__________
❏	❏	Laundry supplies	____	__________	__________	__________
❏	❏	__________	____	__________	__________	__________

* See pages 15 and 16 for precise sizes

PLANNING GUIDES — DETAILED BY ROOM

S. Mud Room

Dominant Color(s): ____________________

Need	Have	Item	#	Size	Color	Style
Furniture:						
❑	❑	Bench	____	________	________	________
❑	❑	Cabinet	____	________	________	________
❑	❑	________	____	________	________	________
❑	❑	________	____	________	________	________
❑	❑	________	____	________	________	________
Lighting:						
❑	❑	Ceiling/wall lamps	____	________	________	________
❑	❑	Cabinet top lamp	____	________	________	________
❑	❑	________	____	________	________	________
Flooring:						
❑	❑	Area rug	____	________	________	________
❑	❑	Floor mat	____	________	________	________
❑	❑	Tile/sheet goods	____	________	________	________
❑	❑	________	____	________	________	________
Windows:						
❑	❑	Curtains/rods	____	________ *	________	________
❑	❑	Blinds/shades	____	________ *	________	________
Accessories:						
❑	❑	Wall hooks	____	________	________	________
❑	❑	Wall racks	____	________	________	________
❑	❑	Wall hangings	____	________	________	________
❑	❑	________	____	________	________	________
❑	❑	________	____	________	________	________
Other:						
❑	❑	________	____	________	________	________
❑	❑	________	____	________	________	________
❑	❑	________	____	________	________	________

* See pages 15 and 16 for precise sizes

PLANNING GUIDES — DETAILED BY ROOM

T. Basement

Dominant Color(s): ______________________

Need	Have	Item	#	Size	Color	Style
Furniture:						
❑	❑	Work bench	____	________	________	________
❑	❑	Shelving	____	________	________	________
❑	❑	Storage cabinets	____	________	________	________
❑	❑	Chairs	____	________	________	________
❑	❑	Game table	____	________	________	________
❑	❑	________	____	________	________	________
❑	❑	________	____	________	________	________
Lighting:						
❑	❑	Ceiling/work lamps	____	________	________	________
❑	❑	________	____	________	________	________
Other:						
❑	❑	________	____	________	________	________

U. Garage

Dominant Color(s): ______________________

Need	Have	Item	#	Size	Color	Style
Furniture:						
❑	❑	Shelving	____	________	________	________
❑	❑	Storage cabinets	____	________	________	________
❑	❑	Work bench	____	________	________	________
❑	❑	________	____	________	________	________
❑	❑	________	____	________	________	________
Other:						
❑	❑	Fire extinguisher	____	________	________	________
❑	❑	Wall hooks	____	________	________	________
❑	❑	House/car tools	____	________	________	________
❑	❑	Gardening tools	____	________	________	________
❑	❑	________	____	________	________	________
❑	❑	________	____	________	________	________

PLANNING GUIDES — DETAILED BY ROOM

V. Patio/Porches

Dominant Color(s): ____________________

Need	Have	Item	#	Size	Color	Style
Furniture:						
❑	❑	Outdoor seating	____	____________	____________	______________
❑	❑	Patio table/chairs	____	____________	____________	______________
❑	❑	Serving cart	____	____________	____________	______________
❑	❑	____________	____	____________	____________	______________
❑	❑	____________	____	____________	____________	______________
❑	❑	____________	____	____________	____________	______________
Appliances:						
❑	❑	Outdoor grill/tools	____	____________	____________	______________
❑	❑	____________	____	____________	____________	______________
Other:						
❑	❑	Log holder	____	____________	____________	______________
❑	❑	Planters	____	____________	____________	______________
❑	❑	Hose/rack	____	____________	____________	______________
❑	❑	Doormat	____	____________	____________	______________
❑	❑	____________	____	____________	____________	______________
❑	❑	____________	____	____________	____________	______________

W. Outside Touches

Dominant Color(s): ____________________

Need	Have	Item	#	Size	Color	Style
❑	❑	Mailbox	____	____________	____________	______________
❑	❑	Door knocker/bell	____	____________	____________	______________
❑	❑	Name/address plate	____	____________	____________	______________
❑	❑	Planters	____	____________	____________	______________
❑	❑	Window boxes	____	____________	____________	______________
❑	❑	Doormat	____	____________	____________	______________
❑	❑	____________	____	____________	____________	______________
❑	❑	____________	____	____________	____________	______________
❑	❑	____________	____	____________	____________	______________

PLANNING GUIDES — DETAILED BY ROOM

X. Extra Room #1

Dominant Color(s): ____________________

Need	Have	Item	#	Size	Color	Style
Furniture:						
❏	❏					
❏	❏					
❏	❏					
❏	❏					
❏	❏					
❏	❏					
❏	❏					
❏	❏					
❏	❏					
❏	❏					
❏	❏					
Lighting:						
❏	❏					
❏	❏					
❏	❏					
❏	❏					
Windows:						
❏	❏			*		
❏	❏			*		
❏	❏			*		
Other:						
❏	❏					
❏	❏					
❏	❏					
❏	❏					
❏	❏					
❏	❏					

* See pages 15 and 16 for precise sizes

PLANNING GUIDES — DETAILED BY ROOM

Y. Extra Room #2

Dominant Color(s): ______________________

Need	Have	Item	#	Size	Color	Style
Furniture:						
❑	❑					
❑	❑					
❑	❑					
❑	❑					
❑	❑					
❑	❑					
❑	❑					
❑	❑					
❑	❑					
❑	❑					
❑	❑					
Lighting:						
❑	❑					
❑	❑					
❑	❑					
❑	❑					
Windows:						
❑	❑			*		
❑	❑			*		
❑	❑			*		
Other:						
❑	❑					
❑	❑					
❑	❑					
❑	❑					
❑	❑					
❑	❑					

* See pages 15 and 16 for precise sizes

PLANNING GUIDES — DETAILED BY ROOM

Z. Extra Room #3

Dominant Color(s): ______________________

Need	Have	Item	#	Size	Color	Style
Furniture:						
❑	❑	________	___	________	________	________
❑	❑	________	___	________	________	________
❑	❑	________	___	________	________	________
❑	❑	________	___	________	________	________
❑	❑	________	___	________	________	________
❑	❑	________	___	________	________	________
❑	❑	________	___	________	________	________
❑	❑	________	___	________	________	________
❑	❑	________	___	________	________	________
❑	❑	________	___	________	________	________
❑	❑	________	___	________	________	________
Lighting:						
❑	❑	________	___	________	________	________
❑	❑	________	___	________	________	________
❑	❑	________	___	________	________	________
❑	❑	________	___	________	________	________
Windows:						
❑	❑	________	___	________ *	________	________
❑	❑	________	___	________ *	________	________
❑	❑	________	___	________ *	________	________
Other:						
❑	❑	________	___	________	________	________
❑	❑	________	___	________	________	________
❑	❑	________	___	________	________	________
❑	❑	________	___	________	________	________
❑	❑	________	___	________	________	________
❑	❑	________	___	________	________	________

* See pages 15 and 16 for precise sizes

Planning Guides

Section II

Detailed By Category

PLANNING GUIDES — DETAILED BY CATEGORY

1. Furniture

For: Living Room • Family Room • Study/Home Office • Foyer • Halls

Need	Item	Total #	Room Codes*
❑	Sofas	______	______
❑	Love seats	______	______
❑	Upholstered chairs	______	______
❑	Ottomans	______	______
❑	Side chairs	______	______
❑	Coffee tables	______	______
❑	Side tables	______	______
❑	End tables	______	______
❑	Sofa back tables	______	______
❑	Lamp tables	______	______
❑	TV cabinets/stands	______	______
❑	Bookcases	______	______
❑	Shelf units	______	______
❑	Display cabinets	______	______
❑	Storage cabinets	______	______
❑	Desk/chair	______	______
❑	Bench	______	______
❑	Game table/chairs	______	______
❑	File cabinets	______	______
❑	______	______	______
❑	______	______	______

*** Room Codes:**

A. Living Room	H. Pantry/Utl Cl	O. Bath #3	V. Patio/Porch
B. Dining Room	I. Master Bedroom	P. Bath #4	W. Outside
C. Family Room	J. Bedroom #2	Q. Upstairs Hall	X. Extra Room #1
D. Study/H. Office	K. Bedroom #3	R. Laundry Room	Y. Extra Room #2
E. Foyer	L. Bedroom #4	S. Mud Room	Z. Extra Room #3
F. Hallway	M. Master Bath	T. Basement	
G. Kitchen	N. Bath #2	U. Garage	

1. Furniture (cont.)

For: Dining Room

Need	Item	Total #	Room Codes*
❑	Dining table	______	______
❑	Dining chairs	______	______
❑	Side chairs	______	______
❑	Sideboard	______	______
❑	Hutch	______	______
❑	Serving cart	______	______
❑	Counter stools	______	______
❑	______	______	______
❑	______	______	______
❑	______	______	______

For: Bedroom

Need	Item	Total #	Room Codes*
❑	Beds/headboards	______	______
❑	Bureaus (his)	______	______
❑	Bureaus (hers)	______	______
❑	Bedside tables	______	______
❑	Blanket chests	______	______
❑	TV stand	______	______
❑	______	______	______
❑	______	______	______
❑	______	______	______
❑	______	______	______

*** Room Codes:**

A. Living Room	H. Pantry/Utl Cl	O. Bath #3	V. Patio/Porch
B. Dining Room	I. Master Bedroom	P. Bath #4	W. Outside
C. Family Room	J. Bedroom #2	Q. Upstairs Hall	X. Extra Room #1
D. Study/H. Office	K. Bedroom #3	R. Laundry Room	Y. Extra Room #2
E. Foyer	L. Bedroom #4	S. Mud Room	Z. Extra Room #3
F. Hallway	M. Master Bath	T. Basement	
G. Kitchen	N. Bath #2	U. Garage	

1. Furniture (cont.)

For: Kitchen

Need	Item	Total #	Room Codes*
❑	Table/chairs	________	________
❑	Storage cabinets	________	________
❑	Counter stools	________	________
❑	________	________	________

For: Pantry/Utility Closet • Laundry Room • Mud Room

Need	Item	Total #	Room Codes*
❑	Shelving	________	________
❑	Storage cabinets	________	________
❑	Bench	________	________
❑	________	________	________

For: Basement • Garage • Patio/Porches

Need	Item	Total #	Room Codes*
❑	Shelving	________	________
❑	Storage cabinets	________	________
❑	Work bench	________	________
❑	Chairs	________	________
❑	Game table	________	________
❑	Outdoor seating	________	________
❑	Serving cart	________	________
❑	________	________	________
❑	________	________	________

*** Room Codes:**

A. Living Room	H. Pantry/Utl Cl	O. Bath #3	V. Patio/Porch
B. Dining Room	I. Master Bedroom	P. Bath #4	W. Outside
C. Family Room	J. Bedroom #2	Q. Upstairs Hall	X. Extra Room #1
D. Study/H. Office	K. Bedroom #3	R. Laundry Room	Y. Extra Room #2
E. Foyer	L. Bedroom #4	S. Mud Room	Z. Extra Room #3
F. Hallway	M. Master Bath	T. Basement	
G. Kitchen	N. Bath #2	U. Garage	

PLANNING GUIDES — DETAILED BY CATEGORY

2. Lighting

Need	Item	Total #	Room Codes*
❑	Table lamps	______	______
❑	Floor lamps	______	______
❑	Wall lamps	______	______
❑	Ceiling lamps	______	______
❑	Picture lamps	______	______
❑	Desk lamps	______	______
❑	Chandeliers	______	______
❑	Sconces	______	______
❑	Cabinet top lamps	______	______
❑	Task area lights	______	______
❑	Bedside lamps	______	______
❑	Bureau lamps	______	______
❑	Work lamps	______	______
❑	______	______	______
❑	______	______	______
❑	______	______	______
❑	______	______	______
❑	______	______	______
❑	______	______	______
❑	______	______	______
❑	______	______	______
❑	______	______	______

*** Room Codes:**

A. Living Room	H. Pantry/Utl Cl	O. Bath #3	V. Patio/Porch
B. Dining Room	I. Master Bedroom	P. Bath #4	W. Outside
C. Family Room	J. Bedroom #2	Q. Upstairs Hall	X. Extra Room #1
D. Study/H. Office	K. Bedroom #3	R. Laundry Room	Y. Extra Room #2
E. Foyer	L. Bedroom #4	S. Mud Room	Z. Extra Room #3
F. Hallway	M. Master Bath	T. Basement	
G. Kitchen	N. Bath #2	U. Garage	

PLANNING GUIDES — DETAILED BY CATEGORY

3. Flooring

Need	Item	Total #	Room Codes*
❑	Carpets	______	______
❑	Area rugs	______	______
❑	Tiled areas	______	______
❑	Sheet goods areas	______	______
❑	Runners	______	______
❑	Floor mats	______	______
❑	Door mats	______	______
❑	______	______	______

Rug size summary —

Room#	Rug#	Size Needed	Color/Style
______	______	______	______
______	______	______	______
______	______	______	______
______	______	______	______
______	______	______	______
______	______	______	______
______	______	______	______
______	______	______	______
______	______	______	______
______	______	______	______
______	______	______	______
______	______	______	______

*** Room Codes:**

A. Living Room	H. Pantry/Utl Cl	O. Bath #3	V. Patio/Porch
B. Dining Room	I. Master Bedroom	P. Bath #4	W. Outside
C. Family Room	J. Bedroom #2	Q. Upstairs Hall	X. Extra Room #1
D. Study/H. Office	K. Bedroom #3	R. Laundry Room	Y. Extra Room #2
E. Foyer	L. Bedroom #4	S. Mud Room	Z. Extra Room #3
F. Hallway	M. Master Bath	T. Basement	
G. Kitchen	N. Bath #2	U. Garage	

PLANNING GUIDES — DETAILED BY CATEGORY

4. Window Treatments (See pages 15 and 16 for precise sizes)

Need	Item	Total #	Room Codes*
❑	Drapes	______	______
❑	Valances	______	______
❑	Curtains	______	______
❑	Blinds	______	______
❑	Drapery rods	______	______
❑	Curtain rods	______	______
❑	______	______	______

Shade/blind size summary—

Room#	Window#	Size Needed	Color/Style
______	______	______	______
______	______	______	______
______	______	______	______
______	______	______	______
______	______	______	______
______	______	______	______
______	______	______	______
______	______	______	______
______	______	______	______
______	______	______	______
______	______	______	______
______	______	______	______
______	______	______	______

*** Room Codes:**

A. Living Room	H. Pantry/Utl Cl	O. Bath #3	V. Patio/Porch
B. Dining Room	I. Master Bedroom	P. Bath #4	W. Outside
C. Family Room	J. Bedroom #2	Q. Upstairs Hall	X. Extra Room #1
D. Study/H. Office	K. Bedroom #3	R. Laundry Room	Y. Extra Room #2
E. Foyer	L. Bedroom #4	S. Mud Room	Z. Extra Room #3
F. Hallway	M. Master Bath	T. Basement	
G. Kitchen	N. Bath #2	U. Garage	

PLANNING GUIDES — DETAILED BY CATEGORY

5. Electronics/Appliances

Need	Item	Total #	Room Codes*
❑	Television sets	_______	_______
❑	VCRs	_______	_______
❑	Audio systems	_______	_______
❑	Telephones	_______	_______
❑	Answering machines	_______	_______
❑	Fax	_______	_______
❑	Computer system	_______	_______
❑	Clock radios	_______	_______
❑	Refrigerator	_______	_______
❑	Cook top/range	_______	_______
❑	Oven	_______	_______
❑	Compactor	_______	_______
❑	Washer	_______	_______
❑	Dryer	_______	_______
❑	Microwave	_______	_______
❑	Toaster oven	_______	_______
❑	Toaster	_______	_______
❑	Food processor	_______	_______
❑	Blender	_______	_______
❑	Coffeemaker	_______	_______
❑	Vacuum	_______	_______
❑	Iron	_______	_______
❑	Outdoor grill	_______	_______
❑	_______	_______	_______

*** Room Codes:**

A. Living Room	H. Pantry/Utl Cl	O. Bath #3	V. Patio/Porch
B. Dining Room	I. Master Bedroom	P. Bath #4	W. Outside
C. Family Room	J. Bedroom #2	Q. Upstairs Hall	X. Extra Room #1
D. Study/H. Office	K. Bedroom #3	R. Laundry Room	Y. Extra Room #2
E. Foyer	L. Bedroom #4	S. Mud Room	Z. Extra Room #3
F. Hallway	M. Master Bath	T. Basement	
G. Kitchen	N. Bath #2	U. Garage	

PLANNING GUIDES — DETAILED BY CATEGORY

6. Bedding & Linens

Need	Item	Total #	Room Codes*
❑	Mattresses/box springs	______	______
❑	Pillows	______	______
❑	Sheets	______	______
❑	Pillowcases	______	______
❑	Blankets/quilts	______	______
❑	Mattress/spring covers	______	______
❑	Bedspreads/coverlets	______	______
❑	Dust ruffles	______	______
❑	Shams	______	______
❑	Throw pillows	______	______
❑	Dresser mats	______	______
❑	Table mats	______	______
❑	Tablecloths	______	______
❑	Placemats	______	______
❑	Napkins	______	______
❑	Patio table set	______	______
❑	Bath towels	______	______
❑	Hand towels	______	______
❑	Washcloths	______	______
❑	Bath mats	______	______
❑	Kitchen hand towels	______	______
❑	Dish towels	______	______
❑	Aprons	______	______
❑	Pot holders	______	______
❑	______	______	______

*** Room Codes:**

A. Living Room	H. Pantry/Utl Cl	O. Bath #3	V. Patio/Porch
B. Dining Room	I. Master Bedroom	P. Bath #4	W. Outside
C. Family Room	J. Bedroom #2	Q. Upstairs Hall	X. Extra Room #1
D. Study/H. Office	K. Bedroom #3	R. Laundry Room	Y. Extra Room #2
E. Foyer	L. Bedroom #4	S. Mud Room	Z. Extra Room #3
F. Hallway	M. Master Bath	T. Basement	
G. Kitchen	N. Bath #2	U. Garage	

PLANNING GUIDES — DETAILED BY CATEGORY

7. Kitchenware

- Servingware...................... use list in Section G on page 71
- Flatware .... use list in Section G on page 71
- Cookware .... use list in Section G on page 71
- Utensils .... use list in Section G on page 72
- Linens .... use list in Section G on page 72
- Other .... use list in Section G on page 72

Need	Item	Total #	Room Codes*
❑			
❑			
❑			
❑			
❑			
❑			
❑			
❑			
❑			
❑			
❑			
❑			
❑			
❑			
❑			
❑			
❑			

*** Room Codes:**

A. Living Room	H. Pantry/Utl Cl	O. Bath #3	V. Patio/Porch
B. Dining Room	I. Master Bedroom	P. Bath #4	W. Outside
C. Family Room	J. Bedroom #2	Q. Upstairs Hall	X. Extra Room #1
D. Study/H. Office	K. Bedroom #3	R. Laundry Room	Y. Extra Room #2
E. Foyer	L. Bedroom #4	S. Mud Room	Z. Extra Room #3
F. Hallway	M. Master Bath	T. Basement	
G. Kitchen	N. Bath #2	U. Garage	

PLANNING GUIDES — DETAILED BY CATEGORY

8. Accessories

Wall Hangings for:

- ❑ Living Room.......................... Use list in Section A on page 58
- ❑ Dining Room.......................... Use list in Section B on page 61
- ❑ Family Room.......................... Use list in Section C on page 64
- ❑ Study/Home Office.......................... Use list in Section D on page 67
- ❑ Foyer.......................... Use list in Section E on page 68
- ❑ Hallway.......................... Use list in Section F on page 68
- ❑ Kitchen.......................... Use list in Section G on page 70
- ❑ Master Bedroom.......................... Use list in Section I on page 75
- ❑ Bedroom #2.......................... Use list in Section J on page 78
- ❑ Bedroom #3.......................... Use list in Section K on page 81
- ❑ Bedroom #4.......................... Use list in Section L on page 84
- ❑ Master Bathroom.......................... Use list in Section M on page 86
- ❑ Bathroom #2.......................... Use list in Section N on page 87
- ❑ Bathroom #3.......................... Use list in Section O on page 88
- ❑ Bathroom #4.......................... Use list in Section P on page 89
- ❑ Upstairs Hall.......................... Use list in Section Q on page 90

Fireplace Area for:

- ❑ Living Room.......................... Use list in Section A on page 59
- ❑ Family Room.......................... Use list in Section C on page 65

Freestanding Decor Items for:

- ❑ Living Room.......................... Use list in Section A on page 59
- ❑ Family Room.......................... Use list in Section C on page 65
- ❑ ____________________ ____________________

Tabletop Items for:

- ❑ Living Room.......................... Use list in Section A on page 58
- ❑ Dining Room.......................... Use list in Section B on page 61
- ❑ Family Room.......................... Use list in Section C on page 64
- ❑ Study/Home Office.......................... Use list in Section D on page 67
- ❑ ____________________ ____________________

8. Accessories (cont.)

<u>Tabletop Items for (cont.):</u>

- ❑ Foyer .... Use list in Section E on page 68
- ❑ Kitchen .... Use list in Section G on page 70
- ❑ Master Bedroom .... Use list in Section I on page 75
- ❑ Bedroom #2 .... Use list in Section J on page 78
- ❑ Bedroom #3 .... Use list in Section K on page 81
- ❑ Bedroom #4 .... Use list in Section L on page 84
- ❑ Upstairs Hall .... Use list in Section Q on page 90

<u>Bathroom Accessories for:</u>

- ❑ Master Bathroom .... Use list in Section M on page 86
- ❑ Bathroom #2 .... Use list in Section N on page 87
- ❑ Bathroom #3 .... Use list in Section O on page 88
- ❑ Bathroom #4 .... Use list in Section P on page 89

<u>Other Accessories for:</u>

- ❑ Pantry .... Use "other" list in Section H on page 73
- ❑ Laundry Room .... Use list in Section R on page 91
- ❑ Mud Room .... Use list in Section S on page 92
- ❑ Garage .... Use "other" list in Section U on page 93
- ❑ Patio/Porch .... Use "other" list in Section V on page 94
- ❑ Outside .... Use list in Section W on page 94

Need	Item	Total #	Room Codes*
❑	Wastebaskets	______	______
❑	Ashtrays	______	______
❑	Games	______	______
❑	Bedspread racks	______	______
❑	Flashlights	______	______
❑	Fire extinguishers	______	______
❑	______	______	______
❑	______	______	______
❑	______	______	______

8. Accessories (cont.)

Need	Item	Total #	Room Codes*
❑			
❑			
❑			
❑			
❑			
❑			
❑			
❑			
❑			
❑			
❑			
❑			
❑			
❑			
❑			
❑			
❑			
❑			
❑			
❑			
❑			
❑			
❑			

*** Room Codes:**

A. Living Room	H. Pantry/Utl Cl	O. Bath #3	V. Patio/Porch
B. Dining Room	I. Master Bedroom	P. Bath #4	W. Outside
C. Family Room	J. Bedroom #2	Q. Upstairs Hall	X. Extra Room #1
D. Study/H. Office	K. Bedroom #3	R. Laundry Room	Y. Extra Room #2
E. Foyer	L. Bedroom #4	S. Mud Room	Z. Extra Room #3
F. Hallway	M. Master Bath	T. Basement	
G. Kitchen	N. Bath #2	U. Garage	

PLANNING GUIDES — DETAILED BY CATEGORY

9. Storage

Need	Item	Total #	Room Codes*
Bedroom Closets:			
❑	Shelving	______	______
❑	Shoe racks	______	______
❑	Tie racks	______	______
❑	Wall hooks	______	______
❑	Hangers	______	______
❑	Hampers	______	______
❑	______	______	______
❑	______	______	______
❑	______	______	______
❑	______	______	______
❑	______	______	______
❑	______	______	______
❑	______	______	______
❑	______	______	______
❑	______	______	______
❑	______	______	______
❑	______	______	______
❑	______	______	______
❑	______	______	______

*** Room Codes:**

A. Living Room	H. Pantry/Utl Cl	O. Bath #3	V. Patio/Porch
B. Dining Room	I. Master Bedroom	P. Bath #4	W. Outside
C. Family Room	J. Bedroom #2	Q. Upstairs Hall	X. Extra Room #1
D. Study/H. Office	K. Bedroom #3	R. Laundry Room	Y. Extra Room #2
E. Foyer	L. Bedroom #4	S. Mud Room	Z. Extra Room #3
F. Hallway	M. Master Bath	T. Basement	
G. Kitchen	N. Bath #2	U. Garage	

Also see "storage cabinets" and "shelving" listed under Furniture on page 100.

PLANNING GUIDES — DETAILED BY CATEGORY

10. Supplies & Hardware

Need	Item	Total #	Room Codes*

Miscellaneous:

- ❑ Lightbulbs ______ ______
- ❑ Extension cords ______ ______
- ❑ Picture hooks ______ ______
- ❑ Tools ______ ______
- ❑ Screws/nails ______ ______
- ❑ Cleaning supplies ______ ______
- ❑ Paper supplies ______ ______
- ❑ Plastic bags/supplies ______ ______
- ❑ ______ ______ ______
- ❑ ______ ______ ______
- ❑ ______ ______ ______
- ❑ ______ ______ ______
- ❑ ______ ______ ______
- ❑ ______ ______ ______
- ❑ ______ ______ ______
- ❑ ______ ______ ______
- ❑ ______ ______ ______
- ❑ ______ ______ ______
- ❑ ______ ______ ______
- ❑ ______ ______ ______
- ❑ ______ ______ ______
- ❑ ______ ______ ______

*** Room Codes:**

A. Living Room	H. Pantry/Utl Cl	O. Bath #3	V. Patio/Porch
B. Dining Room	I. Master Bedroom	P. Bath #4	W. Outside
C. Family Room	J. Bedroom #2	Q. Upstairs Hall	X. Extra Room #1
D. Study/H. Office	K. Bedroom #3	R. Laundry Room	Y. Extra Room #2
E. Foyer	L. Bedroom #4	S. Mud Room	Z. Extra Room #3
F. Hallway	M. Master Bath	T. Basement	
G. Kitchen	N. Bath #2	U. Garage	

PLANNING GUIDES — DETAILED BY CATEGORY

11. Other

- ❑ Pantry/Utility Closet .... Use list in Section H on page 73
- ❑ Garage .... Use list in Section U on page 93
- ❑ Patio/Porches .... Use list in Section V on page 94
- ❑ Outside Touches .... Use list in Section W on page 94

Need	Item	Total #	Room Codes*
❑			
❑			
❑			
❑			
❑			
❑			
❑			
❑			
❑			
❑			
❑			
❑			
❑			
❑			
❑			
❑			
❑			

*** Room Codes:**

A. Living Room	H. Pantry/Utl Cl	O. Bath #3	V. Patio/Porch
B. Dining Room	I. Master Bedroom	P. Bath #4	W. Outside
C. Family Room	J. Bedroom #2	Q. Upstairs Hall	X. Extra Room #1
D. Study/H. Office	K. Bedroom #3	R. Laundry Room	Y. Extra Room #2
E. Foyer	L. Bedroom #4	S. Mud Room	Z. Extra Room #3
F. Hallway	M. Master Bath	T. Basement	
G. Kitchen	N. Bath #2	U. Garage	

Appendix

Web Sites Worth Visiting

Why use the Internet?

The Internet provides an invaluable resource for most any interior design project. A world of planning tools, ideas, and expert how-to techniques are now at your disposal 24 hours a day, even if you live in the most remote location. Virtually every important home furnishings manufacturer and distributor now provides comprehensive product information on their web sites, many of them with on-line buying options. Add to that the Internet auction sites, letting you buy direct from individuals and antique dealers worldwide, and you have an unprecedented opportunity to truly shop the world, rather than just your neighborhood.

There can also be enormous savings in both time and money. One of the more instructive examples appeared in an article in *The New York Times* on Sunday, April 9, 2000. The article reported on the experiences of a young woman decorating her new Manhattan apartment. She wanted to furnish the place tastefully with antiques and early American oil paintings. After roaming through stores and shops in New York's Upper East Side, she determined that she'd need a budget of close to $50,000 to achieve the effect she wanted, and that didn't even include the paintings.

So she turned to the Internet. To her delight, she found much of what she wanted on the web at enormous savings. Her combined costs for furniture, rugs, home electronics, and accessories came in at just over $10,000—$40,000 less than her original retail estimate!

Many of her purchases were made through web auction sites. Occasionally, if the auction minimum bid wasn't met, she'd call the seller to negotiate a price. In more than 70 separate transactions, she had only three items damaged in shipping, all due to inadequate packing. All were shipped fully insured, however, and she had no losses. Two cautionary notes: to avoid problems, select only sellers that have good reputations (this information is posted by previous buyers, right on the site), and skip over items with unclear photos that make it hard to see the item's detail and condition. Even then, ask lots of questions about the object's condition and the shipping costs that apply.

Throughout, she found the whole experience quite enjoyable, and she reported that the sellers were very helpful and accommodating.

Of course, she didn't buy everything on the Web. She bought lots of her everyday items at Home Depot and at local discount stores. The Web, however, was her principal source for the major decorative items.

With furnishings out of the way, she next began searching for her early American paintings. She used the Web to screen art dealers, determining what was available, where, and at what price. In most cases, she went in person to the galleries to inspect the work and negotiate the final price. Here, too, she saved lots of time and money.

Her bottom line comment about her whole experience shopping on the Internet—"It's analogous to having a global amalgamation of stores right in front of you."

That's the reason it's smart to harness the power of the Internet in all your future decorating projects!

When to use the Internet?

During the planning phase, to stimulate ideas. And during the procurement phase, to find the best sources.

As mentioned previously, just about every housewares and home furnishings supplier now gives their web site address in their ads. And you can use search engines like Yahoo, Excite, Hotbot, Infoseek, Lycos, Ask Jeeves, etc. to find suppliers for just about everything that exists. On these supplier sites, you'll find comprehensive product information, usually far in excess of what even the most experienced retail sales person can tell you. Often you'll find special closeout merchandise not available at retail.

With zillions of web sites out there, and thousands more being added (and/or changed) weekly, it's impossible to provide a comprehensive list of decorating and home furnishings web sites but here are some of my current favorites:

1. Search Engines—to find sites by product category, by company, or by topic:

www.altavista.com	Excellent for exhaustive and precise searches
www.ask.com	Leads you through questions to narrow search
www.dogpile.com	Checks through 13 Web search engines for you
www.excite.com	Good for broad general topics
www.hotbot.com	The search engine of Wired magazine
www.infoseek.com	Produces very accurate and relevant results
www.isleuth.com	Excellent for highly specialized searches
www.lycos.com	Has a good selection of advanced search capabilities
www.metacrawler.com	Great for a quick search of what's out there
www.nlsearch.com	Also searches through periodicals and books
www.yahoo.com	A human compiled directory. . . great for broad topics

2. Associations and Organizations

www.aiaonline.com	American Institute of Architects
www.interiors.org	American Society of Interior Designers

www.asla.org	American Society of Landscape Architects
www.colormarketing.org	Color Marketing Group
www.iida.com	International Interior Design Association
www.nahb.com	National Association of Home Builders
www.nari.org	National Association of the Remodeling Industry
www.nkba.com	National Kitchen & Bath Association
www.nthp.org	National Trust for Historic Preservation
www.nchd.org	National Center for Heritage Development
www.remodelingsource.com	Remodelers Council

3. Decor planning / How-to / What's available

www.askbuild.com	Site of syndicated renovation columnist Tim Carter
www.bhglive	From Better Homes & Gardens, has problem solvers
www.blackanddecker.com	Tools and more
www.decoratewaverly.com	From Waverly Fabrics—includes how to decorate section
www.dresslerstencils.com	Great stencils for decorative painting
www.DYIonline.com	Helps you design everything from kitchens to decks
www.goodhome.com	Lets you experiment with color and style changes
www.hardwareworld.com	Hardware and more
www.homearts.com/shelter	How-to articles, links to mag sites, gallery of homes
www.homedepot.com	Home Depot's site
www.homeportfolio.com	900 design showrooms, over 12,000 premium products
www.hometime.com	Based on the PBS "Hometime" how-to series
www.improvenet.com	Design ideas, products, cost estimates, contractors
www.living.com	Lets you shop by room, housewares department, and style
www.ourhouse.com	An online home improvement warehouse
www.outsideliving.com	Covers lawn, garden and patio supplies—even plants
www.pbs.org	Leads you to the "This Old House" PBS-TV series
www.pella.com	Windows and more
www.shopnow.com	Links to vendors
www.thisoldhouse.org	Links to "This Old House" magazine

4. Auction sites

www.amazon.com	It's not just books anymore!
www.ubid.com	Online auction
www.ebay.com	The original—start searching here
www.firstauction.com	America Online's resident auction site

www.onsale.com	Combines a superstore and auction site—electronics specialty
www.sothebys.com	Fine furniture and decorative arts from Sotheby's and beyond
www.unclaimedbaggage.com	You could find a lost treasure for peanuts

5. Department and Discount Stores

www.bloomingdales.com	Bloomingdale's, Inc.
www.costco.com	Costco Warehouse Club
www.isn.com	Internet Shopping Network
www.jcpenney.com	JC Penney Company, Inc.
www.kmart.com	K-Mart
www.macys.com	Macy's
www.samsclub.com	Sam's Club Warehouse Stores
www.servicemerchandise.com	Service Merchandise Co.
www.spiegel.com	Spiegel Catalog, Inc.
www.target.com	Target Stores
www.wal-mart.com	Wal-Mart Stores, Inc.

6. Furniture (also see sites in sections 3, 4 and 5 above)

www.ethanallen.com	The Ethan Allen Collection
www.furniture.com	Comes with a 30-day money back guarantee
www.workbenchfurniture.com	Inexpensive contemporary furniture
www.crateandbarrel.com	Inexpensive furniture and housewares for casual living
www.spiegel.com	Spiegel Catalog, Inc.
www.thomasville.com	High-end, period Thomasville Furniture

7. Fabrics

www.decoratewaverly.com	From Waverly Fabrics—includes how to decorate section
www.surefit.com	Ready-made slipcovers by mail

8. Window Treatments

www.blindstogo.com	Blinds and shades from Blinds To Go
www.kirsch.com	Window fashion ideas from Kirsch

9. Home Electronics and Appliances

www.bestbuy.com	Computer stuff
www.circuitcity.com	Order online and pick up locally, if you want
www.electronics.net	Electronics.net

www.jandr.com	J&R Consumer Electronics
www.radioshack.com	RadioShack

10. Kitchenware

www.chefscatalog.com	Chef's Catalog
www.cooking.com	Cooking.com
www.digitalchef.com	Digital Chef, Inc.
www.williams-sonoma.com	Williams-Sonoma

11. Bedding and Linens

www.linensnthings.com	For bath and bedroom
www.thecompanystore.com	For bed linens and more

12. Lamps —

www.lampstore.com	Hundreds of in-stock lamps,free shipping
www.rejuvenation.com	Reproduction lamps and fixtures

13. Your Favorite Web Sites

www.	
www.	
www.	
www.	
www.	
www.	
www.	
www.	
www.	

www.	
www.	
www.	
www.	
www.	
www.	
www.	
www.	
www.	
www.	
www.	
www.	
www.	
www.	
www.	
www.	
www.	
www.	

Notes / Good Sources

Notes / Good Sources

Notes / Good Sources

Notes / Good Sources